Edith Wharton at Home

Life at The Mount

Edith Wharton at Home

Life at The Mount

Richard Guy Wilson
Foreword by Pauline C. Metcalf
Photographs by John Arthur

THE MONACELLI PRESS

Copyright © 2012 The Monacelli Press LLC
Text copyright © 2012 Richard Guy Wilson
Photographs copyright © 2012 John Arthur (as noted on page 187)
Photographs copyright © 2012 David Dashiell (as noted on page 187)

Published in the United States by The Monacelli Press LLC

Library of Congress Cataloging-in-Publication Data
Wilson, Richard Guy, 1940-
 Edith Wharton at Home : Life at The Mount / Richard Guy Wilson ;
Foreword by Pauline C. Metcalf ; Photography by John Arthur. --
First Edition.
    pages cm
 ISBN 978-1-58093-328-5 (hardback)
1. Lenox (Mass.)--Biography. 2. Mount, The (Lenox, Mass.) 3. Wharton,
Edith, 1862-1937--Homes and haunts--Massachusets--Lenox. I. Title.
 F74.L57W57 2012
 974.4'1--dc23
                          2012010514

10 9 8 7 6 5 4 3 2 1

First edition

Designed by Abigail Sturges
Printed in China

www.monacellipress.com

CONTENTS

ACKNOWLEDGMENTS

During the fall of 1968 at the University of Michigan, Professor Leonard K. Easton, a leading architectural historian, assigned *The House of Mirth* in a class on turn-of-the-century American architecture. Although I had struggled with an excerpt from *Ethan Frome* years earlier in high school, Edith Wharton was largely unknown to me. The novel with its architectural settings enthralled and helped direct me toward writing my Ph.D. dissertation, "Charles F. McKim and The American Renaissance." In April 1970 while researching in McKim's papers at the Library of Congress, I came across a three-page single-spaced carbon copy of a "memorandum" in his letter books. It was clearly about architecture and the role of interior decoration, but there was no name attached to it. Then I held the pages up to a lighted window and found the faint traces in pencil of "to Mrs. Wharton" at the top. A few months later, in a small cache of Edith Wharton's letters at the New York Public Library, I found her note to McKim asking him to review the manuscript of what became *The Decoration of Houses*. That summer while researching the various McKim, Mead & White houses in the Berkshires, I visited The Mount while it was still part of Foxhollow School. This would be the first of many visits over the years.

Discoveries can lead to publications, and, in my case, I initially treated the McKim-Wharton connection in a symposium and publication sponsored by the Victorian Society and edited by Kenneth Ames. This led to my collaboration with Pauline Metcalf on her exhibition and book *Ogden Codman and the Decoration of Houses* (1988–89), in which I treated in much greater detail Edith Wharton's architectural interests. Portions of this book are indebted to my earlier writings and research. Of course I have returned to The Mount many times and watched its changes and participated in some of the events there. I thank John Arthur, who originally thought of the idea of a book on The Mount.

Research for this book has been carried out at many locations, among them the Beinecke Library at Yale University, the major repository for Wharton's papers. Other archives and libraries include the Boston Athenaeum, Historic New England, the Newport Historical Society, The Redwood Library, Avery Fine Art and Architectural Library at Columbia University, the Metropolitan Museum of Art, the New York Public Library, The New-York Historical Society, and the University of Virginia.

Since the 1960s, interest in Edith Wharton has expanded greatly, with many books, articles, and dissertations devoted to all aspects of her life. Many of these are mentioned in the notes, but in particular I want to acknowledge several upon whom I have depended: R. W. B. Lewis's pathbreaking study *Edith Wharton: A Biography*

Edith Wharton at her desk in the library at The Mount, c. 1904.

(1975), Eleanor Dwight's *Edith Wharton: An Extraordinary Life* (1994), and Hermione Lee's *Edith Wharton* (2007). Also to be acknowledged is the late Louis Auchincloss, whose writings beginning in the 1950s helped to revive interest in Wharton's literary and social role. Special thanks to Stuart Siegel for sharing his research on F. L. V. Hoppin with me. Thank you also to Richard and Linda Jackson and Cornelia Gilder for their writings and research on the Berkshires. At The Mount I have had the help of many individuals, and I want to acknowledge Thomas S. Hayes and Stephanie W. Copeland, past executive directors, and Susan Wissler, the current executive director. Mention must also be made of many individuals who have served on the board and made major contributions, including Amy Bess Miller, Jonas Dovydenas, Ann Fitzpatrick Brown, Lila Berle, and Catha Rambusch.

Staff at The Mount over the years have contributed great research and helped me. They include David Dashiell, Erica Donnis, Elizabeth Stone, Nynke Dorhout, David H. Bennett, Wendy Baker, and Diane Dirkes. The late Scott Marshall, who worked for many years at The Mount, produced the wonderful historic structures report *The Mount: Home of Edith Wharton* (1997), which has been invaluable for this book.

Pauline C. Metcalf

"A Very Charming Estate" was the headline referring to The Mount in *The Berkshire Topics* of September 1904. "Its strikingly tasteful architectural lines . . . [give it] an air of stateliness and dignity, yet an air of simplicity . . . that stifles the slightest suggestion of pretence or simulation." Henry James, a frequent visitor, hailed The Mount as "a delicate French chateau mirrored in a Massachusetts pond . . . a monument to the almost too impeccable taste of its so accomplished mistress." The house, its interiors, and its gardens reflected the total involvement of Edith Wharton, who dedicated herself to their creation. It was also where she wrote several of her early literary masterpieces. In spite of its significance, The Mount came close to demolition in the late 1970s.

Unfortunately it was only for a short period, not even a full ten years (1902–1911), that The Mount provided Edith Wharton with the solace she craved. Since that time, The Mount has gone through a number of incarnations with several owners, among them, Foxhollow, a girls' school that folded in 1976. The property lay abandoned and shrouded in neglect, its once magnificent gardens obscured by overgrowth until 1980, when Edith Wharton Restoration was founded to restore and preserve it. A number of local residents, headed by Lila W. Berle, a graduate of Foxhollow, recognized not only the national importance of preserving Wharton's legacy, but also its potential to become a cultural center for the arts, a retreat for experiencing what Edith Wharton referred to as "the complex art of civilized living."

Since that time, much has happened to the property. Starting with an extensive historic structures report written by the late Scott Marshall, a most dedicated and passionate Wharton scholar and friend of The Mount, the house and gardens have been restored to enable visitors to understand the estate as the embodiment of Edith Wharton's philosophy of architecture, landscape, and interior decoration. The entrance drive and gardens, originally created with the assistance of Edith's niece, Beatrix Farrand, have been returned to their original splendor. While the house does not contain any of the original furnishings (there are only a few period photographs to document its appearance), Edith Wharton's personal library of 2,700 volumes has returned. Since the bequest to the son of the great historian Sir Kenneth Clark, the library was owned by a book dealer in Britain. The acquisition by The Mount is especially significant. Not only does it provide a reminder of the soul of its original occupant, with books returning to their former place on the library shelves, it reinforces the unspoken language of rooms.

I was first drawn to The Mount in the late 1970s, when, as a student at the Columbia Program of Historic Preservation, I visited the house while doing research

The Mount — Residence of Mr. E. R. Wharton, Lenox, Mass.

Tinted postcard of The Mount, seen from the Flower Garden.

on Ogden Codman. Despite its shabby state, with crumbling plaster and badly stained exterior, I was captivated by its inherently elegant presence and realized the extent to which it demonstrated the tenets of Wharton and Codman's 1897 bible of good taste, *The Decoration of Houses*. Phrases stating that the treatment of the interior ought "to be based on right proportion, balance of door and window spacing and simple unconfused lines" were evident even in its forlorn state.

Richard Guy Wilson's inclusive description of Edith Wharton and The Mount has brought together the numerous complexities that are part of the story of its creation, including details of the many players involved. Not only does he shed light on the building of the estate, but ultimately its significance in the life and legacy of this multitalented woman.

As of this writing, there is still much to be done to ensure the future of the historic property and fulfill the mission of Edith Wharton Restoration. The most recent project has been the furnishing of Wharton's bedroom and boudoir with pieces from a Newport collection and the installation of new curtains in the original red toile. Next will be the restoration and adaptive reuse of the stable as a cultural center dedicated to the exploration and performance of the arts so key to the life and work of this remarkable woman.

This book is written among many tributes in recognition of the 150th anniversary of Edith Wharton's birth.

CHAPTER 1

Finding Her Way

"It was only at The Mount that I was really happy," Edith Wharton wrote of her years in Lenox in the Berkshire Hills of western Massachusetts.[1] She poured heart and soul into the design of The Mount, beginning in 1901, and she resided there until 1911. The great novelist Henry James, a frequent visitor, summed up its importance: "No one fully knows our Edith who hasn't seen her in the act of creating a habitation for herself."[2] Another friend, Marion (Mrs. Gordon) Bell, wrote: "Here was Edith Wharton the artist, content with nothing less than the best in gardening, the cooking, the furnishing and housekeeping of the place."[3] The house, its interiors, its gardens, and the entire estate were in many ways Edith Wharton's creation, for she involved herself in every aspect of its design and construction, and it is there that she "came of age" as an author, writing several of the novels that placed her in the front ranks of American writers. She gained the self-confidence to create such masterpieces as *The House of Mirth* (1905) and *The Fruit of the Tree* (1907), and the setting of the Berkshires would continue to reappear in later works, such as *Ethan Frome* (1911), *Summer* (1917), and many short stories.

Edith Wharton liked to write sitting in bed every morning. Her bedroom looked out on the gardens below, and they make an appearance in *The House of Mirth*: "The windows stood open to the sparkling freshness of the September morning, and between the yellow boughs she caught a perspective of hedges and parterres leading by degrees of lessening formality to the free undulations of the park."[4]

The Mount plays a central role not simply as the home of a writer where great works were created, but also as a demonstration of a side of Edith Wharton that is less well known, her involvement in architecture, interior design, and landscape

Edith Wharton, c. 1897.

Edward Harrison May,
Edith Newbold Jones,
1870.

gardening. The importance of buildings began early, for as she wrote in *A Backward Glance* (1934): "My photographic memory of rooms and houses . . . was from my earliest years a source in inarticulate misery, for I was always vaguely frightened by ugliness."[5] Many people are surprised to learn that her first published book was *The Decoration of Houses* (1897), co-written with the architect and interior designer Ogden Codman. In this book, which had a major impact on both sides of the Atlantic, Wharton and Codman attempted to reform American interior design, which they called "a varnished barbarism," by a "return to architectural principles . . . of the past."[6] While The Mount was under construction, Wharton published *Italian Villas and Their Gardens*, which had a great influence on garden design, specifically on those at The Mount. Architecture, decoration, and landscape played a central role in Wharton's fiction, for, as she wrote in the short story "The Angel at the Grave," "Each organism draws from its surroundings." The setting is important, and for the main character, Paulina Anson "the house possessed her," much in the same way, Edith would recall The Mount as "my first real home."[7] In her Yale University honorary doctorate talk of 1923, subsequently published in *The Writing of Fiction*, she observed: "The impression produced by a landscape, a street or a house should always, to the novelist, be an event in the history of a soul."[8]

A product of many forces and individuals, The Mount is an important example of major changes that were taking place in the design world during the late nineteenth and early twentieth century in America. Edith Wharton was part of what might be called an "American Renaissance," and to understand The Mount, her earlier life and culture need to be examined.

Youth

She was born Edith Newbold Jones on January 24, 1862, in New York City. The family had New England origins, but the immediate background was "Old New York," which figured in many of her writings. Her relations bore the names of Rhinelander, Pendelton, King, Schermerhorn, Stevens, Ledyard, and Newbold, and through family marriages she had connections with all of New York society. Her parents, George Frederic Jones and Lucretia Rhinelander Jones, were considered "old wealth," meaning not rich as in the sense of the "new money" of robber barons like the Vanderbilts, who in the late 1870s began to make a splash in New York and later Newport. An indication of her parents' social striving, Edith's baptism took place at Grace Episcopal Church, which had more social standing than Calvary Episcopal, which her mother routinely attended. And the saying "keeping up with the Joneses" has often been attributed to her family. Edith's youth was sheltered and, combined with a diminutive stature and a mother who seemed not to care for her, a time of trial. Her mother nicknamed her "Puss" or "Pussy," and the names stayed with her for the remainder of her life. In her fiction mothers frequently appear as cold and manipulative. Her father, who was involved in finance and suffered some reversals, emerges as the caring parent, and she adored him. But she also recognized his ineffectual and indecisive characteristics, and he became a partial model for many of her male characters, such as Lawrence Selden of *The House of Mirth* and Newland Archer of *The Age of Innocence*. Because of financial problems, her father took the family to Europe where living was cheaper, and Edith spent the years between 1866 and 1872 and 1880 and 1882 in France and traveling.[9]

View from the terrace over the meadow to Laurel Lake.

Pencraig, the Jones summer cottage in Newport.

When not in Europe, the family spent the summers in Newport, Rhode Island, which from the 1850s onwards became one of the social hot spots for wealthy New Yorkers. The Jones house, Pencraig (c. 1865), located on the Narragansett Bay side of Aquidneck Island, was in an exposed timber frame style popular in Newport at the time and sometimes called "the Stick Style."[10] Edith would later recall the summers in Newport as consisting of tedious driving up and down Bellevue Avenue with her mother making calls; attending picnics, archery matches, and dances; and, more nostalgically, taking quiet drives in the country.

That children reject the taste of their elders has become axiomatic, and it was true with Edith. Visually and intellectually, she rejected the architecture, decoration, and art of her parents. In a memoir she recalled her earliest "visual impressions" and how she came to "hating certain rooms in a London house of my aunt's," because of "the ugliness."[11] Later in her life she would look back with a certain nostalgia at her parents' taste, but it was an innocent age, not one for emulation. In her autobiography, she notes "the shameless squalor of the purlieus of the New York dock in the seventies," in contrast with "the glories of Rome and the architectural majesty of Paris." She discovered in her father's library a respite from New York's "mean monotonous streets without architecture, without great churches or palaces, or any visible memorials of an historic past." When she was past seventy, she still remembered the "intolerable ugliness of New York, of its untended streets and narrow houses so lacking in external dignity, so crammed with smug and suffocating upholstery." Certainly it was her parents' house on West 23rd Street she recalled: an interior filled with overstuffed furniture, printed and flocked wallpaper and upholstery; a virtual archive of everything she would dismiss in *The Decoration of Houses*. Like much of New York, the house was constructed of brownstone, an effect she characterized as a "universal chocolate-coloured coating of the most hideous stone ever quarried."[12] She described her mother as a "born shopper" who filled the drawing room with bric-à-brac, and stuffed the gilded cabinets with old lace and painted fans.[13] These decorative objects appeared in her fictions of Old New York, and Edith herself, in spite of her tensions with her mother, was always a great shopper.

A somewhat shy young girl given at times to depression and anxiety, Edith never attended school. Her education came through tutors and governesses and her father's library. In her memoirs, the library and the books it contained play a central

Living room of the Jones house in New York.

*Left: Edith Newbold
Jones.
Right: Edward R.
Wharton.*

role in her fascination with storytelling, words, and especially books on art and architecture. Her father gave her John Ruskin's *The Stones of Venice* and Walter Pater's *Renaissance Studies*, and from his library and in living abroad, she glimpsed the possibility of a different environment.[14] A bit later she discovered James Fergusson's *History of Architecture:* "It shed on my misty haunting sense of the beauty of old buildings the light of historical and technical precision, and cleared and extended my horizon."[15]

Young ladies of her social standing were expected to marry, and after several unsuccessful courtships, Edith met Edward R. Wharton, known as Teddy, a socially prominent and handsome Bostonian. They were married in 1885. An indication of her inexperience, she recounts when a few days prior to the wedding, she asked her mother what to expect and received as a reply: "You've seen enough pictures & statues in your life. Haven't you noticed that men are—made differently from women?"[16] Henry James termed their marriage "an almost—or rather an utterly—inconceivable thing."[17] Speculation abounds about their relationship and the obvious intellectual and apparent sexual incompatibility. Edith and Teddy did grow apart over the years, but they also lived, traveled, and remodeled and built two houses together. Teddy's father suffered from what was called "melancholia" and was confined to an asylum, where he committed suicide in 1891. Beginning about 1901, Teddy began to exhibit similar traits. Edith, in spite of recurring bouts of headaches and depressions, began to develop her literary interests with poems and short stories and published her first story in 1890.

Teddy and Edith Wharton were well-off or "comfortable," but not wealthy. Teddy, who never worked, subsisted on an allowance from his mother, expecting to inherit a vast sum. Edith inherited money in a series of trusts that accumulated over time. In the 1880s she was gaining about $9,000 a year, and in 1901 after the death of her mother she was receiving over $22,000 from trusts alone. She also made some money from her writing beginning in the mid-1890s, though initially it was minimal. Her income increased substantially when *The House of Mirth* became a best seller in 1905.

Initially Edith and Teddy set up housekeeping in Newport in Pencraig Cottage, a wooden, gingerbread festooned house across the street from her mother's, where she remodeled a portion of the interior and worked on the gardens. They lived there from June to February and then traveled abroad. Beginning in 1889, they spent part of the winter in New York in a small house they bought on Park Avenue. Travel abroad would continue, and Teddy certainly gained something from it, but he never developed Edith's consuming interests in art and architecture.

Edith (upper right) and Teddy (lower right), with Lucretia Rhinelander Jones (center), Miss Edgar, and Hoyt Gould.

Drawing room,
884 Park Avenue,
New York.

In 1888 the Whartons joined James Van Alen on a three-month Mediterranean cruise on the yacht *Vanadis*, viewing the remains of ancient civilizations. Van Alen was a wealthy New Yorker whose Newport house, Wakehurst, was a center of social life; he was a cousin-in-law of Edith's and would remain a close friend for years. Her diary of the trip shows her already extensive knowledge and sophistication about art and architecture. Of the Temple of Concord at Girgenti she observed: "If arches had not been cut through the walls of the cella, it would still present a complete skeleton of a Doric temple, and yet be more like the real things than a skeleton, . . . gone are the sculptures of pediments and metopes, gone is the outer coating of polished marble— dust overlaid with fair colours . . . How the architect would have shuddered to think that his raw masses of sandstone would remain exposed to the eyes of future critics."[18]

Although Edith became an ardent Francophile, Italy and the Renaissance architecture, art, and gardens of the fifteenth and sixteenth centuries initially attracted her, and she explored and began writing short pieces that were published. Very important to her literary and artistic development were friendships with Vernon Lee (nee Violet Paget) and later with Bernard Berenson. Berenson, born in Lithuania, grew up in Boston and attended Harvard, where he fell under the spell of Charles Eliot Norton and Isabella Stewart Gardner, the latter of whom helped support him in Italy, where he became the leading scholar of Italian Renaissance art.[19] Through the French novelist Paul Bourget, whom she entertained in Newport in 1893 during his American tour, she met Vernon Lee, who was the center of the Anglo-American colony in the hills of Florence. A noted author and aesthete, Lee would be very important in

21

John Singer Sargent,
Egerton Leigh
Winthrop*, 1901.*

introducing Edith to the concept of empathy in art and also the special genius of the Italian garden.[20]

The American Renaissance

One of the striking passages in Wharton's memoir *A Backward Glance* concerns a major change that occurred in that "stagnant air of old New York . . . the dust of new ideas," when "men of exceptional intelligence" emerged. She names Charles Follen McKim, Stanford White, Richard Morris Hunt, Egerton Winthrop, and Ogden Codman. They were part of an artistic and cultural revolution of the late nineteenth and early twentieth century known as the American Renaissance.[21]

The term "American Renaissance" has come to mean the identification by many Americans with the European Renaissance, and in particular Italy of the fifteenth and sixteenth centuries. Bernard Berenson prefaced his first book on Italian painting of 1894 with an observation on the great sympathy existing between America and the Renaissance: "The spirit which animates us was anticipated by the spirit of the Renaissance . . . That spirit seems like the small rough model after which ours is being fashioned."[22] The American Renaissance meant the appropriation as background for the new American wealth of Italian palazzos, Georgian country houses, French tapestries and furniture, old master paintings. It also meant the training of American painters, sculptors, and architects abroad at the École des Beaux-Arts or in imitations of European schools at home. Charles McKim, of the New York firm of McKim, Mead & White, explained that "as many European countries had gone to Rome to understand the splendid standards of Classic and Renaissance art, so must we become students, and delve, bring back and adapt to conditions here, a ground work on which to build."[23] The American Renaissance reordered culture, and a shift occurred in visual and physical form: the brown and ponderous decades of the 1860s, 1870s, and 1880s gave way to the light colors and classical forms of the 1890s and 1900s. Dark, overelaborate, and ahistorical furniture of Belter or Herter Brothers—and of the parlors of Edith's youth—was replaced by simple and gracefully curving reproductions of Louis XVI or American Georgian.

Although the origins of the American Renaissance can be traced back to the 1870s, it was the 1893 World's Columbian Exposition and its White City, or Court of Honor, in Chicago that brought it fully into public view. Here constructed almost overnight was a classical ensemble that would impact American architecture for the next four decades, issuing in a major reorientation in city planning and public buildings. Whether the Whartons actually visited the White City remains unclear, but

Walter Gay, Drawing Room, Egerton Leigh Winthrop House*, c. 1900.*

they would have known of it from the many press reports. Beginning in 1894 Edith participated in fundraising activities for Charles McKim's American School of Architecture in Rome, which later became the American Academy in Rome.[24]

One of Edith Wharton's bright lights in the new air blowing through New York was Egerton Winthrop, who became a mentor and remained a very close friend until his death in 1916. Winthrop, born in 1839, was nearly twice her age. He took her under his wing, introduced her to advanced French literary naturalism and also to Darwin, Spencer, and Huxley.[25] An intellectual, Winthrop also was fascinated by society. Edith would claim an indifference to the pretense of society, but subliminally—perhaps—Winthrop suggested to her the possibilities of that society's setting for fiction. Winthrop, his interiors, and his taste would serve as a model for her fictional society gossip Sillerton Jackson, who appears in *The Age of Innocence* and the novellas that make up *Old New York*.

A widower, lawyer, cosmopolitan, and connoisseur of paintings, furniture, and literature, Winthrop had lived in Paris for many years. His house on East 33rd Street in New York had been designed in 1878–79 by Richard Morris Hunt, the first American to attend the École des Beaux-Arts, in an austere French Second Empire style. The interiors reflected Winthrop's taste and involvement; he "had gone so far as to import from France every article of furniture used—even the papier-mâché ornamentations of the walls and ceiling," along with mantels, tapestries, and paintings. The rooms were some of the earliest in America by the Parisian decorating firm of Jules Allard & Sons. These interiors were well known in stuffy New York; they appeared in *Artistic Houses*, a remarkable compendium of taste, as a rare example— in 1883–84—of Louis XVI style and a "persistent determination to reproduce in all respects the forms, color and feeling of a particular era." The author of *Artistic Houses* speculated that Winthrop said to himself: "I will create a Louis Seize room that shall reproduce the impression of an absolute original. It is the kind of room that I prefer to all others, and neither diligence nor expense shall be spared in pursuit of my object."[26] Mixed in with this were a few well-selected examples of American antiques. For Edith, Winthrop's interiors were a revelation: "Educated taste had replaced stuffy upholstery and rubbishy 'ornaments' with objects of real beauty in a simply designed setting." But she also noted his interests could become "trivial" and "frivolous," that emptiness could yawn in the middle of such fastidious taste.[27]

Winthrop certainly spurred Edith's interest in art, but she never became a collector. The art that she and Teddy would purchase was to be part of an arranged interior scheme rather than independent works of art. This strategy is evident at The Mount, where the paintings are inset into decorative wall panels. Art would play a constant role in her developing fiction and frequently functioned as an important part of a setting. In *The Age of Innocence*, Ellen Olenska and Newland Archer seek a meeting place at the Metropolitan Museum and they avoid the "popular Wolfe collection" of "anecdotic canvases" for the "Cesnola antiquities," as a more appropriate final rendezvous.[28]

The importance of art and classical taste can be seen in a letter Edith wrote to the editor of the Newport newspaper concerning the problem of school decoration. She admonished the town for not better decorating school rooms: "Beautiful pictures and statues may influence conduct as well as taste," and "We must teach our children to care for beauty before great monuments and noble buildings arise." The connection between well-designed and beautiful houses and civic virtue is a constant theme.[29]

Ogden Codman.

Land's End

In March 1893, with funds from a trust created by a wealthy cousin on her father's side whom she had never met, Edith Wharton purchased Land's End. Located in the southernmost part of Newport on Ledge Road, where Bellevue Avenue turns and shortly becomes Ocean Drive, Land's End was several miles from her mother's house. Edith loved the site with "its windows framing the endlessly changing moods of the misty Atlantic and the night-long sound of the surges against the cliffs." Originally designed for the Boston banker Samuel Gray Ward in 1864 by the architect John Hubbard Sturgis, the house was described by Edith as "incurably ugly."[30] Land's End would be Edith's first major attempt at decoration and becomes a steppingstone to *The Decoration of Houses* and ultimately The Mount.

Edith and Teddy—who was vitally engaged in the project—hired Ogden Codman to remodel the house. Codman had entered their life about 1890, and the three became very close friends. A mutual interest in architecture and decoration drew Edith and Ogden together. He may have helped in some decoration of Pencraig Cottage, though this is unclear. They both loved France, which Edith later in her life would explain as having a "universal existence of taste, and of the standard it creates."[31] Codman personified "taste"; he had an air of cultivation that Edith found compelling, especially in contrast to the typical men of wealth—the Gus Trenors of *The House of Mirth*—who knew art, architecture, or furniture only as a commodity.

Two of Ogden's uncles, Richard Codman, an interior decorator in Boston, and John Hubbard Sturgis, greatly influenced his choice of profession, although he

Land's End, Newport.

rebelled against their tastes, which were of the gaudy Victorian extremes. He spent a year studying at the School of Technology (Massachusetts Institute of Technology) department of architecture, but found it unsatisfactory and withdrew. Two years were spent in an architect's office in Lowell, Massachusetts, and then back in Boston he worked for the furniture making and decorating firm of A. H. Davenport & Co. and for Andrews and Jacques, protégées of H. H. Richardson who designed in the heavy Romanesque manner.

Codman's tastes were different and he struck out on his own, initially in the area of interior decoration. He made friends with the architects Arthur Little and Herbert Browne, who shared his interest in New England architecture of the eighteenth and early nineteenth century, and they became known as "the colonial trinity."[32] Always a social snob and certain of the superiority of his taste, Codman searched for clients among the upper levels of society. He tried making contacts through his family's social connections and visited Newport, where he met the Whartons.[33] Codman typifies the type of male friend that Edith tended to collect and that would remain with her for the rest of her life: charming, of good breeding and background, intelligent with artistic interests, and frequently asexual or bisexual.

Constructed of wood in the so-called "Stick Style," with lots of surface ornament and massive ill-proportioned mansard roofs, Land's End was exactly the sort of house Edith and Ogden would loathe. The renovation involved minor exterior changes, such as stripping away some of the extraneous ornament; extensive work on the grounds; and major interior alterations. The work went on between 1893 and 1897, with the majority of the interior and forecourt done in 1893-94, and the garden and minor interior work done in the next couple of years. On the exterior the house remained awkward; a circular forecourt and hedge added formality to the main approach and masked the service wing. On the garden side, terraces and paths were graded. Wooden trellises, pergolas, columns, and lath niches—drawn from Daniel Marot's book *Das Ornamentwerk*, which Codman owned and also recalling stone niches Edith had recently seen at Vicobello in Siena—masked the rambling house from the formal garden. Edith's niece Beatrix Jones Farrand may have assisted on some of the trellis design, since a rendering attributed to her survives. Edith pointed out the issues to Codman: "It will perhaps be a rather nice question how to 'marry' the pergola with the hedge on the one side and the veranda columns on the other."[34]

Edith and Ogden intended the interior to be a showpiece in the manner of the much-admired rooms of Egerton Winthrop. Land's End is the beginning point for *The Decoration of Houses*; yet seen from the book's vantage point of a few years later and also Edith's lambasting "curtains, lambrequins, jardinières of artificial plants,

Beatrix Farrand, Rendering of rose trellis, Land's End, c. 1893.

*Drawing room,
Land's End.*

Library, Land's End.

wobbly velvet-covered tables littered with silver gew-gaws and festoons of lace on mantelpieces and dressing-tables," the rooms at Land's End retreat into the overdone rococo scrollwork and still-cluttered interiors of the early 1890s.[35] Constrained by the preexisting shell, some rooms, such as the drawing room, appear too low for their breadth, and the proportions are mean. The library had delicate Louis XVI paneling, medallion scrollwork, and leafage, but this was set off with the overstuffed furniture and dark bookcases that would be rejected in *The Decoration of Houses*. A too-heavy and large clock and urns overpower the mantel and the space. Simple eighteenth-century French and Italian furniture occupied the dining and sitting rooms, but the damask wall covering—which Wharton and Codman would soon announce to be unsanitary—had a heavy and bold pattern resembling flock. In both rooms the plaster ceiling lacked any relation to the room below and asserted too much weight.

Entrance Hall, Land's End.

Other rooms were more successful. A former porch off the sitting room was enclosed to make a glazed veranda. With its plain floor covering and elegant wooden furniture, this sitting room was the most relaxed and inviting space in the house. Photographed with "clutter" on the reading table, the residual taste of the earlier decades was still apparent. When Edith was unable to purchase a suitable ceiling in Italy, Codman designed an Adamesque or Pompeian "tent" ceiling, but it was never installed. Her boudoir had simple elongated paneling and toile curtains and upholstery.

The vestibule and entrance hall came very close to what Edith and Ogden advocated in *The Decoration of Houses*: "the vestibule is the introduction to the hall, so the hall is the introduction of the living-rooms of the house; and it follows that the hall must be much more formal than the living rooms." What they especially deplored was the "tendency of recent English and American decoration . . . to treat the hall, not as a hall, but as a living room."[36] Not for Edith and Ogden were the vast informal halls of the shingled cottages of McKim, Mead & White or Richardson further up Bellevue Avenue. The hall at Land's End had white plaster moldings simulating reeds—a popular eighteenth-century motif. The applied cornice and dado gave it an architectural order, while the furniture was sparse and yet elegant, a prelude to the rooms beyond.

Boudoir, Land's End.

Edith's involvement with the remodeling of Land's End was total. She admonished Codman regarding the colors of the library shown in one of his elegant renderings: "Room will suffer very much unless the draughtsman can take off that dark red from the upper part of the panels & make them a uniform pink."[37] The library as constructed followed her colors. Much of the furniture, such as the eighteenth-century Italian chairs in the dining room, was purchased abroad in the next few years in the company of Paul Bourget and his wife. In a sense, the house was never finished. New ideas were introduced, colors changed, the garden altered, or new toile fabrics purchased abroad. And she would run errands for Codman, bringing home from Paris panels and other objects.

The Whartons and Codman visited constantly, dining together at least once and frequently several times a week either in New York or in Newport. Ogden also made some changes to their New York townhouse, a combination of the house they purchased in 1889 and the house next door. The exact extent of Codman's involvement is unclear: drawings exist for integrating the two houses, but apparently the project was never carried out in totality. Codman's hand was evident with the French wallpaper and the architectural fittings on the interior.

The Decoration of Houses

The collaboration on Land's End resulted in the book *The Decoration of Houses* and helped to lead Edith in new directions. In spite of some ongoing depressions and other illnesses, she continued to write, producing several short stories in which architecture figures. Codman was game for thinly veiled parody in print. Her short story collection of 1896, *The Valley of Childish Things, and Other Emblems*, contains ten short fables that reveal her increasing dissatisfaction with Newport and her marriage. A little girl escapes from the valley of childhood and sees the world. When she returns years later, she finds her youthful chums still not grown and most of them "were playing the same old games, and the few who affected to be working were engaged in such strenuous occupations as building mudpies and sailing paper boats." Another fable concerns a lady who needs her house turned around; an architect is engaged who replied: "Anything could be done for money." Codman's bills are parodied: the lady "who enjoyed a handsome income, was obliged to reduce her way of living and sell her securities at a sacrifice to raise money enough for the purpose." In still another fable, the ego of architects comes into question when a "successful architect" appears at heaven's gate and is given as alternatives: "Either we can let the

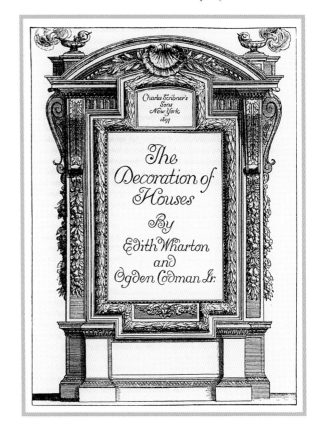

world go on thinking your temple a masterpiece and you the greatest architect that ever lived, or we can send to earth a young fellow we've got here who will discover your mistake at a glance and point it out so clearly to posterity that you'll be the laughing-stock of all succeeding generations of architects." The architect answers, "'Oh well, if it comes to that, you know—as long as it suits my clients as it is, I really don't see the use of making such a fuss.'" The last fable points directly to Codman; he had just finished his first house for Mrs. Charles Coolidge Pomeroy in Newport, a small Colonial Revival house of stucco that local wags christened the "mud palace." Edith's fable recounts the story of a man who wanted to build a temple but could produce only "a mud hut thatched with straw." She ends her fable and short story with a passerby observing: "There are two worse plights than yours. One is to have no god; the other is to build a mud hut and mistake it for the Parthenon."[38]

Architecture is a metaphor in the short story "The Fullness of Life," which suggests increasing marital tensions. "I have sometimes thought," she writes, "that a woman's nature is like a great house full of rooms: there is the hall, through which everyone passes in going in and out; the drawing room, where one receives formal visits; the sitting room, where the members of the family come and go as they like; but beyond that, far beyond, are other rooms . . . and in the innermost room, the holy of holies, the soul sits alone and waits for a footstep that never comes."[39] Certainly a commentary on her marriage, the passage also shows that architecture as a metaphor had distinctly physical connotations and a sexual or erotic dimension.

Wharton's architectural proclivities are evident in letters she wrote to the local Newport newspaper that argued Newport contained a rich heritage of houses from the colonial period: "It is to be regretted that their example has hitherto exercised no influence upon our later local architecture." Paraphrasing in many ways a very short description by Charles Follen McKim twenty years earlier, she argued that American architects ought to be looking at their own past.[40]

Edith and Teddy continued yearly trips to Europe, and she continued to explore different styles and expressions. Many of the illustrations in *The Decoration of Houses* were acquired during their European travels. In England she visited numerous large country houses, such as Wilton and Belton House. Edith's purchases of Italian settecento furniture began then, along with explorations of villas, gardens, and monasteries. These adventures would result in her first novel, *The Valley of Decision* (1902), which was set in Italy in the eighteenth century, and also the books *Italian Villas and Their Gardens* (1904), and *Italian Backgrounds* (1905). Her letters to Codman from Italy were those of the delighted discoverer and serious student. From Parma in 1896 she wrote: "Alas, however, there is apparently no 'call' for anything in architecture later than the 16th century, and all the lovely barocco [sic] fountains, palaces, staircases, and etc. remain unphotographed."[41] From Milan she announced: "I am bringing you a lot of photographs of Mantua which will make you fall down & worship, & then tear your hair out to think you didn't go there. Imagine two or three hundred Villa Madama & Papa Guilo's rolled into one, & you will have a faint, but only *a very faint idea*, of the Palazzo de Te & the Ducal Palace—I never

Edith Wharton, c. 1885–86.

dreamed such splendor was left—you will think nothing of what you have seen elsewhere." Near the end of the letter, she brings up an issue that divided them: he felt that the supreme taste was French and she thought otherwise: "If I could only get you to see that on this side of the Alps the Roman tradition continued unbroken, & that through what you call the barbaric period [middle or dark ages] one may trace the same exquisite refinement & fitness of line and ornament."[42]

For Codman's part, friendship with the Whartons brought him new clients. As he wrote his mother in December 1893: "Who do you suppose I have for a client? Teddy Wharton told me today that Mr. Cornelius Vanderbilt wants to see me at his office at 11:30 tomorrow to talk about his Newport house and he wants me to do part! Just think what a client!!! The richest and nicest of them all . . . I am going to thank Mrs. Wharton who brought this about."[43] Codman designed the upper two floors of the Breakers and through the Wharton connection got other Newport and New York jobs. Through Edith, Codman met McKim, who hired him to decorate the interior of the Frederick Vanderbilt house in Hyde Park and proposed him for membership in the American Institute of Architects. That effort was unsuccessful, but Codman was on his way.[44]

Walter Van Rensselaer Berry.

At some point but certainly by mid-1896, Edith and Ogden agreed to write a book on the principles of interior decoration and architecture. They quickly discovered that books were different from houses, and Edith noted in her autobiography, "Neither of us knew how to write!" Other problems existed as well.[45] Edith took the lead, since she had already published a few short stories, poems, and travel pieces. Codman could write chatty letters but not books, although he undoubtedly thought (as many nonwriters—especially architects—do) a book would be easy: Edith would write down his thoughts. Later they differed on who contributed what, Ogden at one time claiming that it was his work and that Edith simply polished up his sentences.[46] Yet the arrangement of the authors' names and surviving correspondence indicates Edith not only wrote most the book but also contributed many of the ideas.

The writing of *The Decoration of Houses* went on for more than a year, and the book appeared on December 3, 1897. In her autobiography, Edith acknowledged the help of a distant relative, Walter Van Rensselaer Berry. The year before she met Teddy, Edith had fallen in love with Berry, and maybe he with her, but then he retreated. Now he reappeared in Newport, a man of "sensitive literary instincts," who, with a shout of laughter at the lump of the manuscript, replied: "Come, let's see what can be done."[47] She wrote to McKim, probably in January 1897, asking him to read what they had written: "I should not have troubled you about the matter at all, if I had not fancied from some talks we have had together that you felt that there were things which needed saying on this very subject, and had I not hoped that, if Mr. Codman and I could say them in the right way we might, in a slight degree, cooperate with the work you are doing in your Roman academy."[48] McKim reacted enthusiastically to the manuscript, concentrating upon the introduction. Edith reported to Ogden: "I think it would be well in some respects to remodel the Introduction . . . the other chapters he entirely agrees to, which is nice."[49]

The publication process was not without issues. Edith's sister-in-law arranged an entry at Macmillan, and she believed the editor, Mr. Brett, "accepts it positively." A question was raised about the title as "not ambitious enough." Brett wanted to call it *The Philosophy of House—decoration*.[50] Other problems arose as Codman's superior manner offended the publisher. What exactly transpired remains unknown; in *A Backward Glance* Edith claimed Macmillan showed the manuscript to an architect who rejected it with "cries of derision."[51] This was patently false, since Edith had in hand Charles McKim's warm praise of the manuscript. Instead she was probably covering up the vexing problem of Codman's attitude. Apparently he so offended Brett that Macmillan canceled the book. In May 1897, Edith wrote to Ogden: "Before we embark on any other experiments with the book, I am going to make it a condition that you leave the transaction entirely to me."[52]

Scribner's magazine had already published several of her short stories and poems, and she turned to the senior editor Edward Burlingame, who passed the

Daniel Marot, Design for a fountain and trellis, Das Ornamentwerk, *1892.*

manuscript on to William Crary Brownell of the firm's book publishing arm. After some hesitation over the expected audience and sales, they accepted it. Charles Scribner, the publisher, felt it lacked potential, but Burlingame and Brownell wanted to encourage Edith.[53] She showered Brownell with ideas for the book, convincing him that thirty-two plates for illustrations would not be enough. She accosted him in Newport, successfully arguing for fifty-six halftone plates.[54] And she convinced him to have Daniel Berkeley Updike, the Boston arts and crafts printer, both design and print the book. Updike, an old friend of Codman's and a new acquaintance of hers, also designed the title page, drawing inspiration from Codman's favorite source book, Marot's *Das Ornamentwerk.*[55]

Edith's letters reveal the struggle of writing and the problems of collaboration: "I think I have mastered hall & stairs at last, & I should like to see all the French & English Renaissance house plans you have."[56] Later she writes to Codman: "I have finished walls (which will have to be a chapter by themselves preceding the Chps. on openings) & I should like you to read it at once."[57] Peevishly she attacks: "Anytime in the last three months you could have made the whole bibliography in your office in an hour—I suppose now that will have to be left out too. I regret very much that I undertook the book. I certainly should not have done so if I had not understood that you were willing to do half, & that the illustrations & all the work that had to be done with the help of your books were to be included in your half. I hate to put my name to anything so badly turned out."[58] Edith wanted plans in the book, but none appeared. Many more letters attest to the trial of collaboration. By November 1897 Edith's letters grow more positive and galleys were being corrected and the index compiled. Worried about reviews, she hoped that *The Nation* would use Thomas Hastings, a Beaux-Arts trained architect who later designed the New York Public Library. Showing her awareness of the architectural landscape, she added: "In any case Russell Sturgis is not to touch it."[59] Sturgis disliked classicism and certainly would not be kind.

Charles McKim had already given the book his approval. McKim represented, as Edith wrote Ogden, "'the high-water-mark' of criticism in that line in America."[60] McKim argued that Italian Renaissance architecture and its progeny in other countries should be the basis of modern architecture. He quibbled with their assertion that the Italian villa was unsuitable for northern climates and claimed that it could "easily be adapted to modern uses as the type of French and English country houses built after 1600." As an example McKim cited Wheatleigh, a house in Lenox by Peabody & Stearns. France certainly had a "present superiority" in architecture; he had been a student at the Beaux-Arts. He concurred with Edith and Ogden that originality lay not in a "willful rejection of what have been accepted as the necessary laws of the various forms of art . . . but in using them to express new . . . conceptions." McKim more explicitly stated the prospect: "The designer should not be too

Charles Follen McKim.

slavish, whether in the composition of a building or a room, in his adherence to the letter of tradition. By conscientious study of the best examples of classic periods, including those of antiquity, it is possible to conceive a perfect result suggestive of a particular period . . . but inspired by the study of them all." Specific styles should rule, and the beginning point for modern design lay with the study of the past, which was the underlying principle of the American Renaissance.[61]

The emphasis of *The Decoration of Houses* lay with the American Renaissance belief that the level of civilization of a nation, or a people, could be read through the arts and especially architecture. Edith and Ogden argued that interior decoration should be considered a branch of architecture. This is an assertion that each generation seems to discover anew, and while Edith and Ogden rather pretentiously cited in support C. A. d'Aviler's *Cours d'Architecture* (1760) and Isaac Ware's *A Complete Body of Architecture* (1756) as precedents, essentially similar views had been expressed by Andrew Jackson Downing and Marianna Griswold Van Rensselaer.[62] The difference lay with the models chosen, for Edith and Ogden rejected the medieval and turned to the Renaissance. Renaissance Italy, while seen as approaching "modern civilization," was unsuited for northern climates, it returned to the "Roman ideal of civic life: the life of the street, the forum and the baths." Instead, Edith and Ogden cited as models "the French and English styles later developed from it," and particularly the French. The reign of Louis XIV was the great divide: "It is to the school of art founded by Louis XIV and to his magnificent patronage of architects and decorators trained in these schools that we owe the preservation, in northern Europe, of that sense of form and spirit of moderation which mark the great classical tradition." English classic taste they describe as less sure, being "perpetually modified by a passion for . . . 'conveniences' which instead of simplifying life not infrequently tend to complicate it." America had little to commend except the colonial, which was "simply a modest copy of Georgian models." [63]

The opening premise of *The Decoration of Houses* was that room decoration had to be considered as part of the total design of a building. Architectural elements ruled the interior as much as they determined the exterior. Superficial application of ornament derived independently of the structure equated with the unsettled medieval period and barbarianism.[64] High civilization appeared when room decoration became architecture; the Renaissance and the return to classicism was the academic tradition that offered consistency. The book was not just a historical study, but a philosophy and a handbook of do's and don'ts. Wharton and Codman's chapters follow a seemingly practical bent, first the elements of rooms and then the totality. Actually their outline also follows that of both Charles Locke Eastlake's *Hints on Household Taste* (1868) and Clarence Cook's *House Beautiful* (1877), two books that Edith and Ogden despised and whose influence *Decoration* was an attempt to correct. After a historical survey comes chapters on parts of rooms, such as walls, doors, windows, fireplaces, and ceilings and floors, and then specific rooms are treated: entrance and vestibule, hall and stairs, and the others. After a chapter on "bric-à-brac," a conclusion repeats the call to return to architectural principles "based upon common sense and regulated by the laws of harmony and proportion."[65]

While part of their argument was based upon the environmental suitability of French architecture, furniture also played a role. French furniture was adaptable to modern comfort, while older Italian Renaissance furniture lacked ease of sitting.

Wheatleigh, Peabody & Stearns, 1893.

Edith collected Italian eighteenth-century furniture because it was cheap and a variation on the French. The book showed examples of medieval furniture and described them as born of an "unsettled state" of "warfare and brigandage" and "stiff and angular." They had been designed to be transported from castle to castle on muleback. Compared to the medieval chairs were the comfortable and civilized armchairs and *bergères* of Louis XIV, XV, and XVI.[66] Ironically, the tall medieval chairs became the predecessors for the arts and crafts movement and designers such as Gustav Stickley and Frank Lloyd Wright.

The fifty-six illustrations that Edith selected for the book showed their point of view. Sometimes criticized for the depictions of rooms from palaces such as Fontainebleau, Versailles, and Mantua, or grand English houses, the illustrations are frequently devoid of furniture. Individual pieces do appear in plates, but the rooms are shown without furnishings to emphasize the architectural character and the importance of moldings and details. People do not appear, except in two eighteenth-century prints showing a woman in a boudoir and a grand "Salon à l'Italienne" with a cluster of women and men.[67] These photographs supported the thesis that constants or laws of good taste existed with regard to room proportion and furniture form. The nadir of American taste, according to Wharton and Codman, came in the period 1840 to 1890, which they describe as a "confusion resulting from . . . unscientific methods" of "piling up of heterogeneous ornament, [and] a multiplication of incongruous effects." Sometimes called "High Victorian," or what the historian Carroll Meeks has labeled "synthetic eclecticism," it was a period when agitated picturesqueness in buildings and furniture was at its height. Wharton and Codman referred to the overstuffed furntiture as padding fit for "a lunatic's cell" or "dubious eclecticism." American architects had led the way in returning to Renaissance models; now if only American decorators and furniture designers would follow in a "study of the best models" and "true principles," Wharton and Codman asserted that the "notable development" would continue.[68]

The close and scientific observation of interiors and furniture came from Edith's travels and studies in Italy. She

Antechamber in the Palazzo Durazzo, Genoa. Plate 29 of The Decoration of Houses.

had digested as soon as they came out Bernard Berenson's studies of Renaissance painting, which introduced her to the "scientific accuracy" of Giovanni Morelli's methods. "A Tuscan Shrine" of 1895 recounts her discovery—with Teddy—at an obscure monastery of an unknown Giovanni della Robbia terra-cotta through close observation and comparison of small details. Proudly she parades her knowledge of the Morelli-Berenson method: "The perception of differences in style is a recently developed faculty." She aspired to replace the "cultured dilettante" type of art and architectural writing of Symonds and Pater; to become a "scientific critic," and combine "scholarly standards" with "aesthetic sensibility."[69]

A spirit of rediscovered classicism pervades *The Decoration of Houses*. Ruskin and other medievalists are attacked for their promotion of asymmetry. Calling upon the acknowledgement of "all students of sociology," Wharton and Codman claim the "instinct for symmetry . . . is more strongly developed in those races which have reached the highest artistic civilization." The effect of a room is largely the result of proportions and the "distributions of openings." This concern with the impact of form was a direct result of Vernon Lee's influence and the notion of empathy; forms, shapes, and spaces made an impact upon people. Noting "mathematical calculation" and "scientific adjustment of voids and masses," Wharton and Codman dub proportion as "good breeding in architecture." Through a discussion of principles and then specific examples, such as the hall in the Durazzo Palace in Genoa or a drawing room at Berkeley Square, London, the arguments are advanced.[70]

Carved door, Palais de Versailles. Plate 18 of The Decoration of Houses.

The Decoration of Houses gained a somewhat notorious reputation as a decorating manual for the Newport "cottages" commissioned by very rich robber barons. But obviously, neither Wharton nor Codman liked, and indeed they parodied, the high-caloric excesses of Richard Morris Hunt and Allard & Sons' dining rooms at the Vanderbilt-owned Marble House and the Breakers. In the conclusion, they attack the "gilded age" and they claim "the supreme excellence is simplicity." Also, since neither writer had children, their chapter on "The School-Room and Nurseries" has been laughed at. But here is also a clue to their outlook and especially Edith's modern literary naturalism, which would shortly come to the fore in *The House of Mirth* and *Ethan Frome*. People, as she demonstrates in these books, are creatures of their environment; they are formed by it, and they cannot escape it. And in *Decoration* the child's room where education takes place is one of the most important; here is developed the sense of beauty. "Beauty," Wharton and Codman noted, "needs as careful cultivation as the other civic virtues." Art should not be regarded as a thing apart from life, and "the daily intercourse with poor pictures, trashy 'ornaments,' and badly designed furniture may, indeed, be fittingly compared with a mental diet of silly and ungrammatical story-books."[71] Edith certainly remembered her education in her father's library and the importance of that environment.[72]

Reviews were generally positive, even though Edith's fears did come to pass, and *The Nation* critic, probably Russell Sturgis, noted it was "handsome, interesting and well-written," but criticized their reliance upon beauty as the guide.[73] Edith schemed to get other reviews and even suggested to Ogden writing another book, "Garden-architecture." The collaboration of a man and woman was noteworthy to one reviewer: "Many details are discussed which would not have been included if there had been but one author, or two authors of one sex."[74] Several reviewers highly praised the book, but felt the illustrations were a disservice; they were too ornate and "not . . . examples of that simplicity which the text preaches."[75] The reviewer for the *New York Herald* loved it and noted they "also condemn in sweeping terms the glaring faults in decorative art shown in many American houses."[76] Walter Berry, who had helped Edith rewrite the text, contributed a review claiming the book began to repair the damage of Eastlake's *Hints on Household Taste*.[77] The reviewer in *The American Architect and Building News* chided their severe condemnation of current

Lunette figure of a child, possibly St. John the Baptist, in the gallery of The Mount.

Medallion of a Roman emperor, panel above the mantel in Teddy Wharton's den at The Mount.

American design, but claimed: "On the whole, the volume is far ahead of anything of the kind we know of within the last half-century." Nothing was wrong with wealth and taste, for if the wealthy demand good moldings, "in time" they will find their "way to the carpenter-built cottage." [78]

The book sold very well upon first appearance; it was reprinted in England and later in America.[79] It helped change taste in decoration on both sides of the Atlantic. Edith sent copies to English architects and critics she felt might be sympathetic and received friendly replies from W. J. Loftie and Reginald Blomfield. They praised her condemnation of "excessive & unmeaning ornament," and hoped her views would prevail in England as well as in America.[80] For years the book was the bible of good taste in classical decoration, and it had a substantial influence on succeeding books.

The success of the book gave Edith Wharton a new purpose, and she determined to change her life. She found Newport filled with "watering place trivialities." To Codman she wrote: "I wish the Vanderbilts didn't retard culture so very thoroughly. They are entrenched in a sort of thermopylae of bad taste, from which apparently no force on earth can dislodge them."[81] In the fall of 1899 Edith made a visit to the Berkshires to visit Teddy's mother and became entranced. The Whartons rented a house in Lenox for the summer of 1900, and she wrote to Codman: "I am in love with the place—climate, scenery, life & all."[82] The Mount was on the horizon.

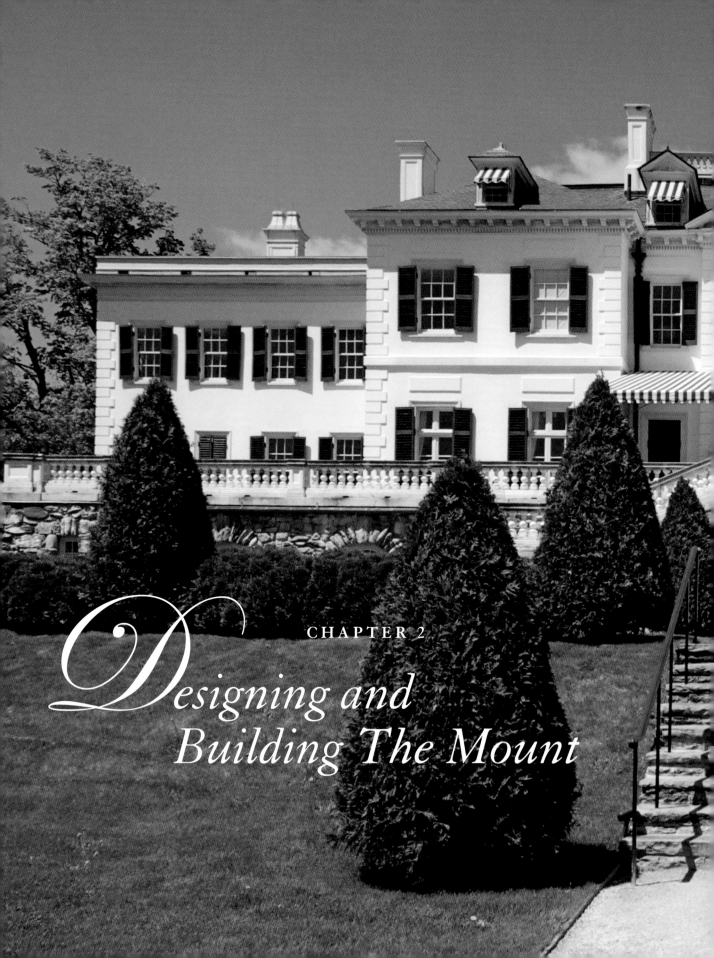

CHAPTER 2

Designing and Building The Mount

nthralled with the Berkshires and the possibilities of a new life, Edith Wharton set about creating the correct house, gardens, and grounds in Lenox. With Teddy's assistance, she would build a country estate that consumed much of her interests between 1900 and 1907. As she created worlds and described the ideal house on paper, now she would try to make a complete physical world. She explained: "On a slope overlooking the dark waters and densely wooded shore of Laurel Lake we built a spacious and dignified house, to which we gave the name of my great-grandfather's place, the Mount."[1]

Negotiations commenced in February 1901 to purchase 113 acres from the Sargent family; later she and Teddy would add more for a total of nearly 150. Edith signed the deed on June 29, and shortly thereafter both Land's End and the New York town house were sold to help pay for the new house and land. An inheritance from her mother, who died in Paris in late June 1901, helped to fund the project, but more money was needed. In February 1902 Edith took out a loan of $50,000 from the Berkshire Savings Bank in Lenox. The property was listed in her name, although Teddy later did sign a guarantee for the mortgage as "husband of said grantor." Altogether, Edith had the funds to create an estate that would meet her discriminating eye.[2]

Lenox Life, the gossipy summer newspaper, announced in late May 1901 that the local builder R. W. Curry was starting to work on a new cottage for Mrs. Edith Wharton, even though she did not yet own the land.[3] Edith signed a contract with Curry in July 1901 with the cost for the mansion estimated at $41,000, the stable at $14,000, and the entrance lodge at $4,580. The final prices were considerably higher

Edith Wharton, c. 1900.

with the house at $57,619.76, the stable at $20,354.46, and the lodge at $5,356.63. This did not include the interior decoration and furnishings or the gardens. The local newspaper followed the course of construction, reporting in August that 160,000 bricks had been delivered from the Nelson Martin Company of Lee and that Barnes and Jenks of Pittsfield was grading the site.[4] Most of the construction on the house took place between July 1901 and September 1902, when the Whartons occupied it, though it took another year to finish all the details; the gardens were not completed until 1905.[5]

Very much in the forefront and indeed the goal of the Whartons' conception of The Mount lay the ideal of the English country house. Wealthy Americans in the late nineteenth century were captivated by the English ideal of a large country estate where family and friends could gather in grand houses that represented generations of status and power. Although Edith and Teddy had visited England earlier, around 1899 they began to focus on English country estates of the so-called Palladian period; in letters home Edith expressed her admiration.[6] English country houses had figured prominently in *The Decoration of Houses* as better suited to the colder climate of the Northern states, specifically those "built in the Palladian manner after its introduction by Inigo Jones." Edith and Ogden noted: "See Campbell's *Vitruvius Britannicus* for numerous examples."[7] Campbell's book would play a

major role in the conception of The Mount. The country house was the traditional seat of political and economic power in England, but this would be very different in the United States, where the money for the grand estates came from other sources, such as finance, real estate, banking, railroads, industry, and mining. Fueling this fascination with country living was the "country life" movement in both countries, with magazines such as the London-based *Country Life* and its New York cousin *Country Life in America* extolling the virtues of the countryside, gardening, horseback riding, and a wholesome lifestyle. The English magazine in particular, with its weekly article on an old English country house, was widely read by wealthy Americans.

This obsession led to the appearance of large houses on substantial acreage across the United States.[8] These were very much in contrast to the resort cottages of Newport, built on relatively small lots. At the summit were the real power houses, such as George Washington Vanderbilt's Biltmore in North Carolina, which sat on thirty thousand acres of land, or the King Ranch in Texas, which was the center of a political dynasty. At a lesser level were houses of substantial size but with more limited acreage. Located in the expanding suburbs of the Northeast and Midwest or in resort areas such as Long Island or the Berkshires, these became known as "country places." Here the owners could play at farming, raise some stock with a hay field

Woodlands,
The Mount.

or two, tend with help flower and vegetable gardens, and, of course, build a substantial house for living and entertaining.

The Mount was a country place. Located about one and one-half miles to the east of Lenox, it was enough removed to imitate a rural setting, but not too distant. A portion of the property was given over to farming, which became Teddy Wharton's domain. Six farm buildings occupied the acreage at the eastern end of the property and were well removed from the house. All of these—a barn, an ice house, a wagon shed, a piggery, and a farmhouse—were built by a prior owner in the 1890s. The Whartons added a henhouse in 1904. The occupant of the farmhouse tended to the animals, cared for the fields of hay, and grew vegetables. The farm's major purpose was to supply the big house with the necessary foodstuffs, and it never produced income for the Whartons.

Another important element of a country place was a substantial woodland. At The Mount oaks and chestnuts shielded the property from the surrounding roads and provided areas for woodland walks. Several wetlands introduced contrast and open views, especially to the east toward Laurel Lake. Paths were laid out and special places created, for instance, a small knoll not too far from the house where the Whartons located a pet cemetery.

Two of the Whartons' dogs—probably Mimi and Toto—pose in the center of perhaps the earliest photograph of the estate, taken in mid-1901. Edith stands on top of a small rocky outcropping with Teddy, appropriately dressed in jacket, vest, and knickers in the foreground. The rocky hill may be the ultimate site for the house, which was deep within the property and well away from the roads.

The Designers

The design of the house and the surrounding estate is a complicated story that involves several characters. Always present, not just as client but as active participant,

Ogden Codman, Preliminary plans for The Mount, 1901.

is Edith Wharton. The exact role of each person is difficult to untangle, since in many cases decisions were made in conversations and on the ground as construction took place.

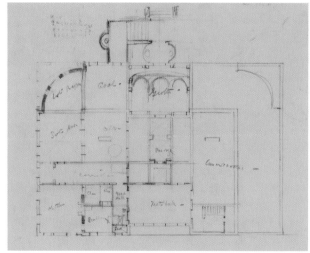

Even before they had decided on a site, Edith approached Ogden Codman in late 1900 to design a house. Codman responded slowly, ultimately producing some very rough plans, which were rejected by the Whartons as too costly. Exactly what next transpired remains unclear. Codman wrote his mother in February 1901: "They [the Whartons] have been fussing about their house so I almost wish I was not going to build it. They do not seem to realize that I am any different from when I did their other house. But they *will learn*. There are times when I fully realize what an idiot Teddy is."[9] The conflict involved several issues. Edith and Teddy felt that since they were both old friends and collaborators, Codman should reduce his fee of 25 percent; he refused. Codman worried over the time the Whartons would demand; he wrote to his mother: "I told them that I was so busy and my work was so scattered I could not be coming up to Lenox all the time."[10] He did have three houses under design in 1900–1, but nonetheless Codman

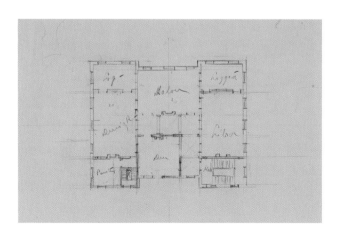

could be leisurely in his work habits. Perhaps more important, Codman worried about his social standing. He convinced himself that Edith's recent short story "The Line of Least Resistance" had alienated those who mattered. As he wrote to his mother: "Mrs. Wally Sloane did not like the story . . . and Mrs. Wharton wrote and apologized for it. Mrs. Sloane is the social queen of Lenox." Filled with infidelity, greed, ignorance, and selfish and shallow characters, the story evidently hit too close to home, for Codman claimed: "Her story about the Sloanes finished her with all the Sloane Vanderbilt hangers on who are now barking at her like a lot of yellow dogs." From Codman's point of view: "I fancy their [the Whartons'] day of useful-ness is over"; and in a letter of a few weeks later he noted: "Poor Miss Pusscod must be replaced while she is still stunned." But he also admitted he wished they had been more upset about his declining to do their house.[11]

In March 1901, Edith wrote to Codman: "It is of much more importance to me that we should maintain our old relation as good friends than risk it by entering on the new and precarious one of architect and client. We are in such close sympathy in things architectural that it would have been a pleasure for me to work with you, but perhaps after all we know each other too well, and are disqualified by that very fact for professional collaboration." She went on to note, "Now that you need not be on your guard against me as a client, perhaps I shall be all the more useful as a friend . . . for it has been a great interest to me to follow your work and try to make people understand what it represents."[12] Codman wrote to his mother the same day: "You will be glad to hear that peace has been declared by the Whartons." A few months later he wrote: "I shall continue to stand up for her as she was kind and helpful to me long ago."[13] One can sense Ogden's shock that Edith would hire another architect, as he realized the chance to do a house with a fully sympathetic client had been lost.

Edith turned to an architect she had known from at least as early as June 1897, Francis (Frank) L. V. Hoppin, and his partner Terrence Koen, who were alumni of McKim, Mead & White.[14] Money is the answer to the obvious question why she approached a relatively young and unknown firm rather than the masters, such as Charles McKim, whom she knew well. By the late 1880s, McKim, Mead & White was focused more on public and commercial buildings and had become extremely selective about residential commissions, working only for the wealthiest clients. Con-temporary with The Mount is Harbor Hill at Roslyn, Long Island, built for Clarence and Katherine Mackay at a cost of $830,000.[15] The Whartons were not in that league, and had Edith approached McKim, he would have declined, perhaps pointing her to Frank Hoppin.

Born in 1867 to a socially distinguished family, Hoppin attended a military training school, then Brown University briefly, and spent two years in the architec-ture program at MIT. Restless, he spent some time in the late 1880s in the McKim, Mead & White office, traveled, and then passed the entrance examination for the

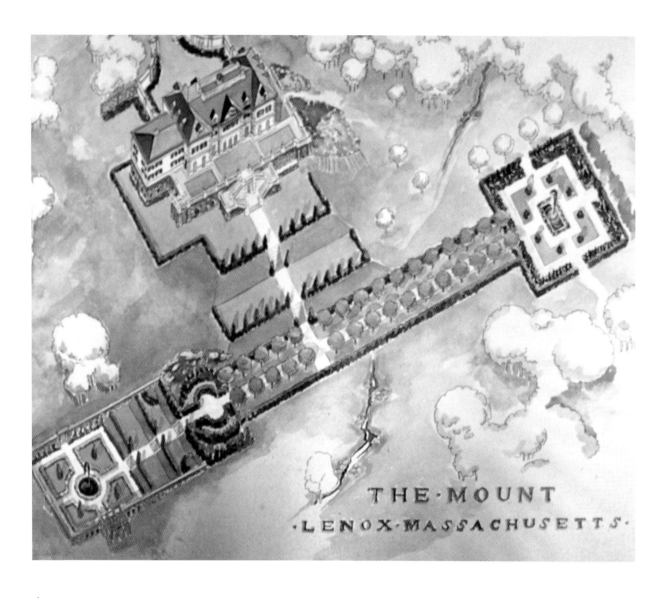

THE·MOUNT
·LENOX·MASSACHUSETTS·

École des Beaux-Arts. He was already an accomplished draftsman and watercolorist, and some of his drawings were published in the preeminent magazine *American Architect and Building News* with the title "Architectural Knockabout."[16] From 1890 to 1894 he was back at McKim, Mead & White, where he achieved a reputation with his splashy renderings of buildings. Charming and socially connected, Hoppin left the firm in 1894 and started his own with Koen. Their office was in the same building in New York as the McKim office, and Hoppin continued to do renderings for the firm over the next several years.

Hoppin & Koen had designed only a few houses when Edith contacted them. Their initial work lay very much in the generic shingled/colonial idiom of the early 1890s and then transitioned to the statelier and classically derived Georgian Revival.

Carol Palermo-Schulze, Bird's-eye view of The Mount and the gardens.

Approach to the house
from the south drive.

The Wharton commission would have been an important job for a young office, although Hoppin undoubtedly recognized that Edith's knowledge and proclivities would not give him a free hand. Codman gleefully reported to his mother in a letter that Hoppin "is having an awful time with the house, which she telegraphs him every day or two and fusses terribly over every detail." Hoppin, according to Ogden, had "been cut down in every way," forced to change the house from brick to stucco over wood and make three sets of plans. "Poor Pussy," he concluded, "is of course very unpopular . . . she has gone out of her way to be rude."[17]

The House

From site selection to design, construction, and furnishings, Edith's involvement was total; in many ways it is her own creation, though with the help of others. The completed house, gardens, and grounds show Edith's three architectural enthusiasms, Italian, French, and English, illuminating the American Renaissance impulse. The approach to the house through the long allée and the dense woods is reminiscent of French country estates near Compiègne or Versailles. The opening or the view onto a broad green lawn upon which the house sits is typically American. Stylistically the house might be called "Georgian," though the English label "Wrenaissance" would be more accurate,

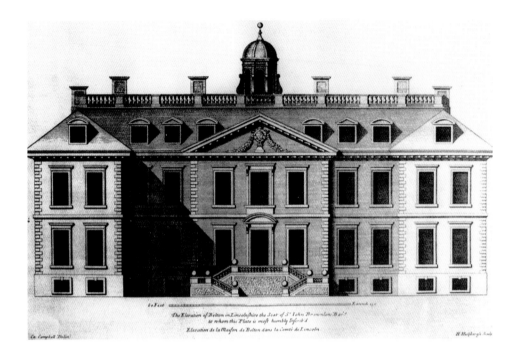

Colin Campbell, Elevation of Belton House, plate 38 in Vitruvius Britannicus, *1715–25.*

indicating its source lies earlier than the Georgian period. Of course the ultimate source for the English model was the Italian villa made serviceable for northern climates recommended by *The Decoration of Houses*. The plan shows French elements; the interior is American in convenience and mechanics, while the decorative scheme recalls French, English, and Italian sources. The terrace and garden were Italian and English in inspiration, and beyond an English-style meadow lay in the distance, an American landscape of lake and mountains.

Sited on a small rocky outcropping near the center of the estate with a view of Laurel Lake about a mile away to the east, the house has three full stories on the west or approach front and only two stories on the east or garden side. The source for the design at least on the east front was identified in a Lenox newspaper article of 1904 as Belton House in Lincolnshire, 1684–86.[18] Edith and Teddy had visited Belton, and apparently she and Ogden had decided upon using it before their dispute. Codman frequently used the H-shaped form in his houses. Hoppin also had designed or had on the drawing board houses based on the Belton prototype.[19] A great house of the Carolinian period, Belton had recently been published in *Country Life* and attributed to Christopher Wren, with carvings by Grinling Gibbons. Belton's elevations were published in Colin Campbell's *Vitruvius Britannicus* (1715–25), but with a terrace staircase that was never built.[20] Smaller than Belton and constructed of white stucco over timber and brick rather than stone, The Mount meets the ground differently from its prototype, which sits on a half basement on a flat site. Placed on the top of a small hill, The Mount rises like a white temple, and the terraces and stairs tie it back to the land.

Codman's rough plans have some relation to Belton, with their H shape and the main staircase pushed into a separate space beside the entry hall. He projected a basement entry continuing through the rock and becoming a grotto on the east side. This would have required expensive rock blasting, which the Whartons could not afford. Codman's main floor, or piano nobile, plan was awkward in circulation with a clumsy L-shaped hall. In many ways, these sketches are inaccurate, and it remains unclear whether Codman was dealing with the actual site of The Mount or a hypothetical location, since his orientation is reversed from the house.

The plan that Edith and Hoppin eventually worked out was ingenious. One entered at the basement level on the west front, progressed up to the piano nobile, and then moved out onto the terrace on the east front. The origin of the plan was undoubtedly French and possibly that of the Petit Trianon at Versailles, 1762–68, by J-A. Gabriel, where the same spatial sequence takes place. The house became a series of layered spaces perpendicular to the main entrance axis. From the ground-level entrance hall, visitors turned right to ascend the stair to the piano nobile. This

View of the east facade of The Mount from the South Garden.

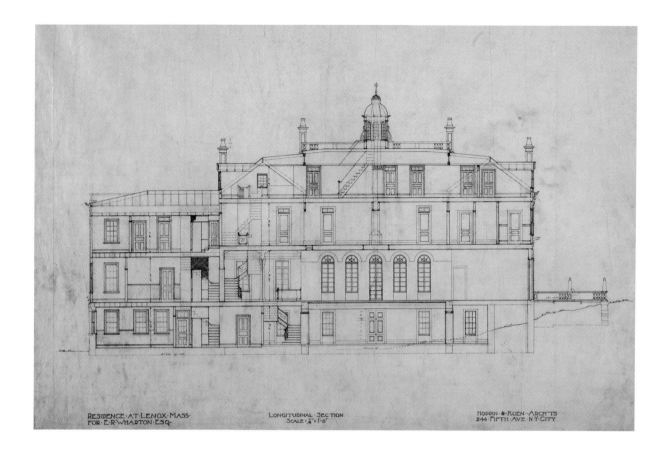

RESIDENCE·AT·LENOX·MASS·
FOR·E·R·WHARTON·ESQ·

LONGITUDINAL·SECTION
SCALE ¼″=1′-0″

HOPPIN·&·KOEN·ARCH'TS
244·FIFTH·AVE·N·Y·CITY

*Hoppin & Koen,
Section, ground-floor
plan, and main-floor
plan, The Mount, 1901.*

floor was a series of enfilade spaces opening onto each other. Across the west front was the cross-axial gallery opening at one end onto the stair hall and at the other end onto the den. In placement and function, the gallery is unique in American country houses of the period. Parallel to the gallery and opening from it was the enfilade of the main living spaces: dining room, drawing room, and library. The same layering of perpendicular spaces occurs on the east front: the terraces as well as the gardens lie across the main central axis of the house.

The service spaces were on the ground floor and in a wing to the south, giving onto the dining room on the main level and the staircase hall on the bedroom floor. On the north the den and library rested directly on the rock.

The third floor has the same layering of space, although a double-loaded corridor or gallery (as labeled on the plan) separates rooms on each side. At the top of the main staircase were three guest bedrooms, the largest facing east and two smaller ones facing west. Teddy's bedroom occupied the center of the block over the drawing room below. He had his own bathroom and dressing room. Edith took up the entire north end with a boudoir, bath, and bedroom. Her suite was the most completely private, with an arch in the corridor-gallery marking the entrance to her domain. The plan can be interpreted as a series of barriers to protect Edith at her work and yet allow the house to function with visitors and guests.

56

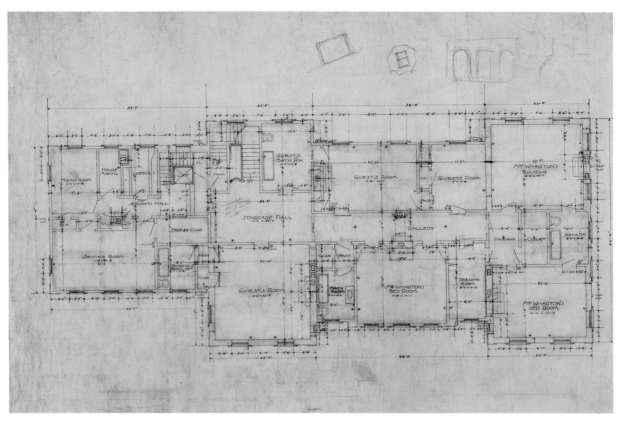

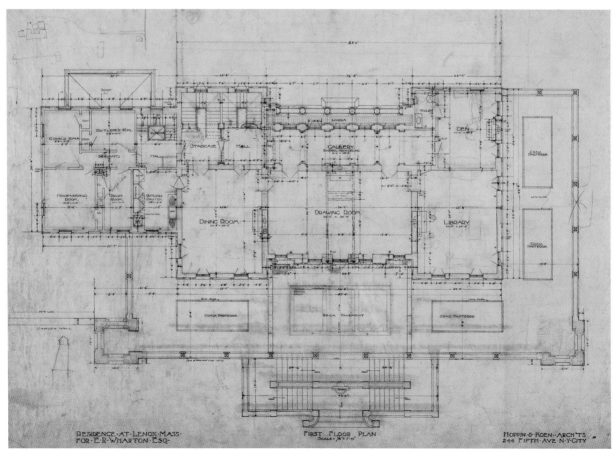

RESIDENCE·AT·LENOX·MASS·
FOR·E·R·WHARTON·ESQ·

FIRST FLOOR PLAN
SCALE ⅛"=1'-0"

HOPPIN & KOEN·ARCH'TS
244 FIFTH·AVE·N·Y·CITY

The service wing to the south contained three levels. On the basement level were the furnace and coal room, the kitchen, the scullery, the laundry, the servants' dining room, the wine closet, a toilet, and back stairs. On the second (main) level were the rooms of the staff who controlled the house: the butler, cook (or chef), and housekeeper's bedrooms, the butler's pantry, and the brush room. On the main bedroom floor were the linen closet, a maid's room, a servant's sewing room, a dress room, and other closets. Edith's maid would have lived here, and within a minute or two she could answer the call bell. The attic level of the main block contained eight servants' bedrooms of various sizes and a bathroom. In 1907 the Whartons engaged Hoppin & Koen to extend the service wing, but the work was never carried out.

Although the exterior of The Mount is derived from several sources, the white walls and green shutters recall early New England houses, as noted by Henry James on one of his visits.[21] The east elevation, or garden-terrace facade, was drawn from Belton but significantly altered. At The Mount the hyphens between the end and central pavilions were reduced, giving the central pavilion a pinched quality. Hoppin also projected a pair of belvedere pavilions on the terrace, but these were never

Above: Front door.

Opposite: Entrance facade.

Overleaf: Sculpture in the forecourt.

built. On the west or entrance front, Hoppin designed a large and elaborate forecourt with French-style wrought-iron gates.[22] This was modified into a smaller space with a verge of turf and two classical statues in niches. Large quoins surround the windows and define the corners of the main block. This ornamental detailing, while simple, has an insistent quality typical of American design of the period, and the quoins, belt courses, dentils, and roof balustrade and cupola appear a little too obvious, too prominent. Symmetry is emphatic; window frames with no openings were inserted to balance real windows. Shutters, not shown on Hoppin's plans, covered the blank openings. Hoppin also projected for the main floor level five round-headed loggia-type windows. They would have more truthfully revealed the interior space of the gallery, but as the drawing shows, they would have appeared incongruous and cramped; Edith told him to change it to three openings.

Entrance hall. A cast of Frederick MacMonnies's Pan of Rohallion *faces the front door.*

The Interior

Initially Edith followed Hoppin's suggestion to hire a French firm to develop the interiors, but she grew dissatisfied with the designs and decided to try Ogden Codman once again. At a New Year's Eve dinner in 1901, Edith broached the subject of decorating the house, and as he wrote to his mother: "I am much pleased as it will put a stop to all talk about our having quarreled."[23] He had already expressed his disapproval of the house after a visit in October 1901: "I am not enthusiastic about their new place but the land and the new buildings have many grave defects. I do not care for Lenox or its society which is rather second rate."[24] By March Codman could report triumphantly: "The Whartons are now domesticated and eat out of my hand," and they had

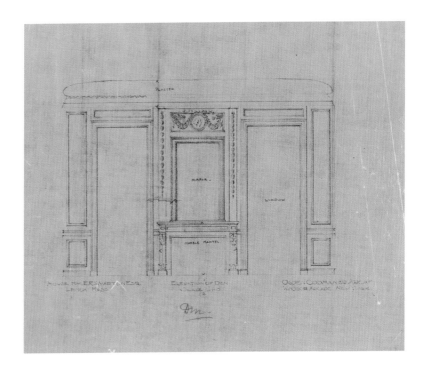

Ogden Codman, Interior elevations. Clockwise from upper left: north wall of Teddy Wharton's den; south and north walls of the dining room; north wall of the library.

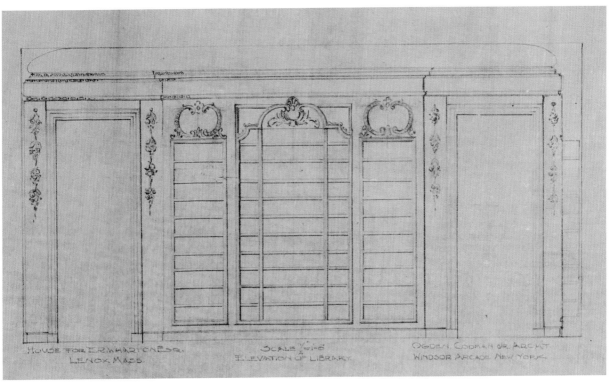

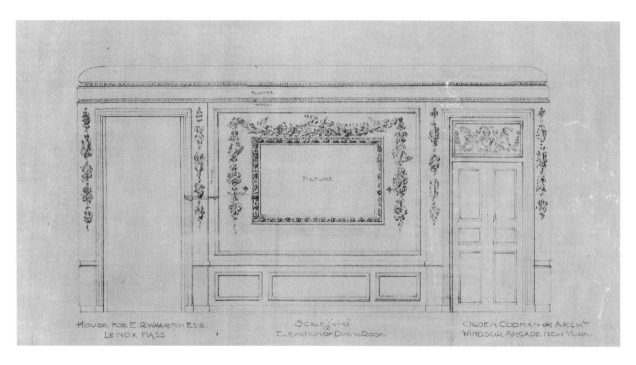

HOUSE FOR E.R.WHARTON ESQ.   SCALE ½=1-0   OGDEN CODMAN JR ARCH'T.
LENOX MASS   ELEVATION OF DINING ROOM.   WINDSOR ARCADE NEW YORK.

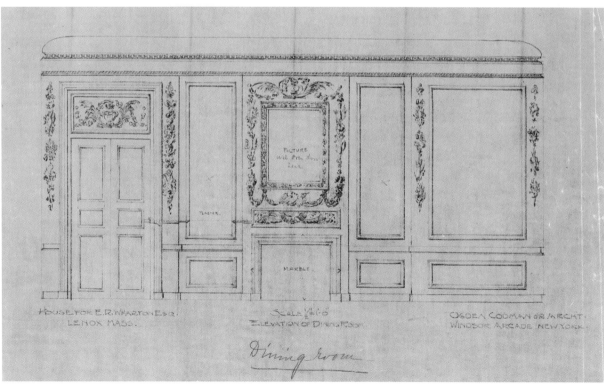

HOUSE FOR E.R.WHARTON ESQ.   SCALE ½=1-0   OGDEN CODMAN JR ARCH'T.
LENOX MASS.   ELEVATION OF DINING ROOM.   WINDSOR ARCADE NEW YORK.

Dining Room

A graceful stair with an ornate cast-iron railing rises to the main floor.

accepted his prices, which were "more expensive than I supposed they would stand for."[25]

Codman—with Edith's advice—did most of the interior. Edith's letters show the usual issues: "Please do it today, for if you haven't already, for I know that there will be pretexts for delay."[26] They argued about decorations, tapestries, and chimney breasts, with Edith citing alternative precedents. The furniture came from Land's End and the New York house, edited by Edith and supplemented by the purchase of some new pieces. The decoration of several of The Mount's rooms, especially Teddy's den and Edith's boudoir, closely followed Codman's designs at Land's End. Codman produced elevations for Teddy's den, Edith's boudoir, the library, the stair hall, and the dining room. It remains unclear what role he played in the entrance hall and the gallery, and the bedrooms.

In her autobiography, Edith recalls being "taxed by my friends with not applying to the arrangements of my own rooms the rigorous rules laid down in *The Decoration of Houses*."[27] The Mount interiors both follow and depart; each room was particularized as to purpose and also personality: "it must be not 'a library,' or 'a drawing-room,' but the library or the drawing-room best suited to the master or mistress of the house which is being decorated."[28]

Entry and Stair Hall

The entrance vestibule retained the air of the proposed grotto: Frederick MacMonnies's garden statue *Pan of Rohallion* (the original of which graced a McKim, Mead & White house in New Jersey) greeted the visitor, the walls were finished in rusticated stucco, and the floor had a reddish and white terra-cotta tile pattern. The stair hall, appropriately separate, as dictated by *The Decoration of Houses*, recalled eighteenth-century Parisian hotels with their smooth masonry courses imitated in stucco and elaborate black wrought-iron balustrades. At the top of the stairs visitors encountered a feature that becomes common throughout The Mount: painted panels set into the wall. These large panels depict elegantly dressed ladies accompanied by a gentleman in a garden setting. Very much French eighteenth century in style, their origin is unknown except that Edith supplied them; they may actually be Italian copies that she purchased. They are topped by elaborate plaster overpanels of flaming urns and a cornice designed by Codman.

The gallery spans the entrance facade of the house and opens to the enfilade of public rooms along the terrace.

The Main Floor

From the stair hall visitors could go straight ahead into the dining room, but more correctly would turn left into the bright gallery with its terrazzo floor and a vaulted ceiling, the most original space in the house. *The Decoration of Houses* had stated that the gallery should "display the art-treasures of the house," but also that spaces used only for passage should have "forcible simple lines, with vigorous massing of light and shade."[29] To discourage lingering, the gallery incorporated architectural details that dramatized movement, and the ceiling compelled attention, as Edith and Ogden claimed it should. Consequently, the furnishings were sparse, three "highly prized Italian console tables," marble columns, vases, and some terracotta statues.[30]

The complex geometry and spare furnishing of the gallery are in keeping with the tenets of The Decoration of Houses.

The drawing room is in the center of the main floor, with three pairs of French doors opening to the terrace. In The Decoration of Houses, *Wharton had observed: "In the country there is nothing more charming than the French doors opening to the floor."*

Throughout the main floor symmetry is in evidence as a guiding principle: false doors or paneling balanced real openings. All the rooms had a luminous quality; ten-foot-high windows opened to provide access to the terrace. The other dominant feature of all the main-floor rooms (and also Edith's boudoir upstairs) was the wall treatment and the use of inset painted panels and large tapestries in the drawing room and library. Wharton and Codman

*The drawing room is
the only room in the
house with an elaborate
plaster ceiling,
composed of foliage
and fruit.*

asserted in *The Decoration of Houses*: "The three noblest forms of wall-decoration are fresco-painting, paneling, and tapestry hangings."[31] Art should be subservient to the architecture of the room and consequently fit into the walls.

"Decorated in English XVII style," as claimed by a local writer, the drawing room could be entered from the gallery, or from the den, dining room, and library.[32] Only one photograph survives from the Wharton tenancy of this room, which was the largest in the house, measuring twenty by thirty-six feet. Here Edith tried to

combine the functions of both a *salon de compagnie* and a *salon de famille*, which she and Codman had argued must be rigorously separated. The furniture was easily movable for conversation, and two large tapestries of mythological subjects dominated the end walls. A few pieces of sculpture were placed about to create an impression. Henry James reported to a friend in October 1904: "Here I am in an exquisite French chateau perched among Massachusetts mountains—most charming ones— and filled exclusively with old French and Italian furniture and decorations."[33]

Teddy Wharton's den, at the northwest corner of the house, featured a carved French rouge *marble mantel.*

At the north end of the gallery, doors opened into Teddy Wharton's den, which could also be accessed from the library, and the terrace. Edith and Ogden noted that the "den" was a modern term and a "descendant" of the smoking-room; it was the personal "lounging room" of the master of the house. Codman carefully designed the room following the dictates of *The Decoration of Houses* with "clear-cut architectural moldings," which would give "dignity to the room and height to the ceiling."[34] Two paintings of mythological subjects were placed in the panels over the doors. Possibly painted by Hoppin, they are fit subjects for the male gaze, depicting a male satyr observing a reclining nude female satyr, and a male satyr playing a pipe to a nude female. No known photographs survive of the den, but it was described as furnished in dark leather upholstery.[35]

The library is paneled in oak with inset bookshelves on three walls. The original furnishings included a bureau-ministre *and a* lit de repos*, both recommended by* The Decoration of Houses.

The library at the northeast corner had perhaps the most attention focused on it. The local gossip sheet claimed: "Mrs. Wharton's literary tastes naturally lead to the conclusion that the library must be one of the interesting rooms in the house."[36] Doors gave onto the terrace on two sides, and the room could also be entered from the den, the gallery, and the drawing room. Louis XVI–style dark oak cases filled with leather-bound sets of books reached to the ceiling on three sides, while a very large set-in tapestry dominated the other. The tapestry was a source of controversy between Edith and Ogden, for she

wrote him: "The change of tapestries you suggest would not do as the two tapestries of which you have sketches are alike in colouring and composition, whereas the one I intended to put in the library is absolutely different."[37] Perhaps an Aubusson tapestry, it depicted a French garden scene similar in view to Versailles. The carving in the overdoor panels and bookcases was more elaborate than suggested in *The Decoration of Houses*. A portrait of her great-grandfather Stevens hung over the mantel. The furniture, such as a *lit de repos* and Louis XVI chairs brought from Newport and two new Regency-style writing tables were background—as stated in *Decoration*—to the books and the conversation that should dominate.[38] Surprisingly, some of the other furniture shown was quite similar to the overstuffed armchairs condemned in *Decoration*. Along the north wall and facing the fireplace stood the writing table, at which Edith posed for a publicity photograph. How much writing was done in the room is debatable, but it served as a place for conversations before and after dinner.

82

In the dining room, inset still life paintings are framed by ornate plasterwork of fruits, vegetables, and flowers interspersed with birds, all designed by Codman in the style of Grinling Gibbons.

The dining room, at the southeast corner of the main block, was the brightest in the house, natural light being important to digestion. To enhance evening artificial illumination, the dining room was painted in white, as proposed in *Decoration*. Access came from the stair halls, the drawing room, and the terrace, while the staff entered at the southwest corner. The floor was terrazzo and continued the flow from the gallery, the stairhall, and the drawing room. As recommended in *Decoration*, the ornament was based on symbols of food and feasting. Carvings of fruit and foliage in high relief, perhaps in reference to Belton, were installed, along with two large painted fruit and flower panels set into the chimney breast and the opposite wall. The dining room chairs were eighteenth-century Italian from Land's End, possessing "wide deep seats so that the long banquets of the day might be endured without constraint or fatigue."[39] The table was a nineteenth-century pedestal type that could be extended. Edith disliked such tables, but she admitted their convenience and, of course, the form would be covered by linens. A Louis XV–style china cabinet and two serving tables made up the rest of the room.

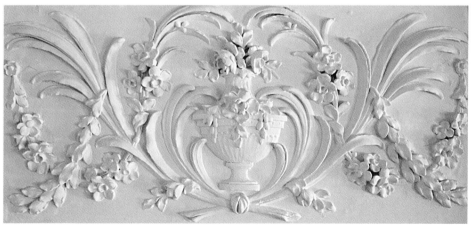

86

The chaise in the
boudoir offers a view
over the gardens.

The Bedroom Floor

The decor of bedroom floor, with the exception of Edith's domain, was much more subdued and indeed sparse. As noted, a hall-gallery bisected the floor with Edith's quarters at the far end. Initially Hoppin and Koen suggested a circular glass opening over the hall to bring light from the cupola down, but Edith drew an 'X' over it on the plan. Consequently the hall was relatively dark. Teddy's bedroom on the east side had an expansive view of the lake and hills beyond. A large mantelpiece dominated one wall and furnishings, though unknown, probably followed the dictates of *Decoration* with space for "the bedstead and its accessories."[40] The three guest rooms of varying sizes were relatively plain with plaster walls. The fireplace mantels received some emphasis. No known photographs of these rooms survive, although they were well furnished. One guest recalled that Edith "showed me my room [and] I remember saying to her: 'What a perfect desk—everything conceivable needed for

Ogden Codman selected
this red toile for Land's
End and used it again at
The Mount.

Overleaf: Newly
installed curtains and
furniture convey the
atmosphere of Wharton's
private domain.

writing is there'; and I can see her little deprecating smile as she answered, 'Oh, I am rather a housekeeperish person.'"[41]

Edith's domain of three rooms plus the shared dressing room with Teddy exemplified some of her decorating ideas. The boudoir was appropriately the most ornate. Edith and Ogden noted it had changed its purpose from its eighteenth-century origins: "though it may preserve the delicate decoration and furniture suggested by its name, such as room is now generally used for the prosaic purpose of interviewing servants, going over accounts and similar occupations." Since it was usually a smaller room, the decoration should be delicate. While Edith and Ogden note that the boudoir could be simple, and as "a rule neither rich nor elaborate," this dictum was certainly not followed at The Mount. The boudoir was ornamented with elaborate plaster moldings, a dominant mantel of red and cream marble, and eight floral paintings set into the walls.[42] The room glowed and the red toile fabric that Codman favored covered the Italian Louis XVI-style furniture.

89

Edith's bedroom across the hall from the boudoir remains a somewhat unknown quantity since no photographs survive; except for servants and Teddy occasionally, no visitors were allowed. The room was light and airy with views out the four windows to the north and east, which took in the gardens and Laurel Lake. Plaster decoration was limited to the cornice. The bedroom furniture would have been simple. Some evidence exists that a wall covering was employed, but if so, that would have gone against the dictates of *The Decoration of Houses*.

Working on a limited budget but striving to keep up with the other large houses in the area, Edith skimped on some aspects of the house, which would later cause problems. Lead was used instead of copper to caulk the roof, and the stucco exterior was inappropriate for the freeze-thaw climate of the area.[43] Whatever questions might be raised about the construction, the house met the Whartons' requirements. As formal design it is impressive: a high point of country house—American or English—organization from the period.

The Grounds and Outbuildings

The Whartons occupied the house in September 1902, but work continued for another year. Codman was among the first visitors. In October 1902, he wrote to his mother that the house looked bad, with the marble floors half finished, the courtyard all out of proportion, and the furniture "awful." Hoppin was "superficial," and with some glee, he claimed the Whartons were unhappy: "The place looks *forlorn* beyond my powers of description." While he expressed some satisfaction with his own work, Codman realized he had made a mistake: "They got in too deeply over their heads, and I am almost sorry I did not come." The landscaping, Codman noted, would "take years and a small fortune . . . to make it even look decent."[44]

 As a "country place," the estate required other elements, such as a formal entrance, a gatehouse, stables, roads, and gardens. The entrance gates designed by Hoppin, composed of wooden pickets and classical piers topped by urn finials, were not completed until 1904. From the entrance the drive opened into a long allée of sugar maples, very French in feeling and most likely designed by Edith's niece

THE STABLE
A Future Restoration Project

Above: Beatrix Jones Farrand, c. 1900.

Opposite: Entrance gate and gatehouse.

Beatrix Jones Farrand in 1901–2. Immediately on the left stood the gatehouse, which housed the estate's superintendent-groundskeeper and head gardener. The small stucco-covered Georgian revival dwelling, designed by Hoppin & Koen, was largely complete by 1902. Heavy quoins and the bright white exterior connect it to the main house

Conveniently next door stood a glass greenhouse with a stucco-covered brick potting shed attached. A small hot-water heater in the cellar of the potting shed provided warmth for the greenhouse during the winter. Greenhouses or conservatories were a necessity on any American country place with aspirations. Behind the greenhouse and gatehouse was an apple orchard.

The stable and carriage barn were about three hundred yards further along the drive and marked the shift to the curving road that led to the main house. Large and expensive in comparison to the house, the stable was Teddy Wharton's domain. As the local newspaper described it, "Mr. Wharton's pride is the stable, which indeed is one of the finest in Lenox. The plan was of his own execution, and architecturally the building is a copy of the stables at Belton."[45] Teddy, who was certainly the source for these comments, overstates a bit his involvement in the design, since Hoppin & Koen were the architects. The reference to Belton is correct; the large Flemish gable on the south front is derived from the Belton stable. However, the brick of Belton became white stucco in Lenox. A massive building, it contained stalls for the horses, a carriage/coach room, a washing room, harness rooms, and other facilities on the ground level with staff quarters above—seven bedrooms, a bath, a servant's sitting room, and trunk storage. As Matilda Gay, wife of the painter Walter Gay, wrote in her journal, the stable "represented an order of things that is rapidly passing."[46] Within a few years, it would also house the Whartons' automobile.

Immediately before the stables on the north side was an extensive kitchen garden divided into different sections by symmetrical pathways, with a pear walk on the north balanced by a grape pergola on the south. Round arched topiary gateways provided access to the garden, which was enclosed by a clipped hedge.[47] Like the main drive, the kitchen garden was designed by Farrand.

The daughter of Edith's older brother Frederic Rhinelander Jones and Mary (Minnie) Cadwalader, Beatrix Jones Farrand became the preeminent American landscape designer of the early twentieth century. Edith quarreled with her brother Frederic, but she developed a very close relationship with his wife and with Beatrix, who became in a sense a sister. Edith's interest in European gardens, especially Italian

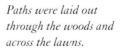

Paths were laid out through the woods and across the lawns.

Opposite: Path to the pet cemetery.

landscapes, certainly helped spur Beatrix's determination to become a landscape gardener. She went on to travel extensively in England and Scotland and viewed the work of landscape gardeners William Robinson and Gertrude Jekyll, whose designs she helped introduce into the United States. In 1899 Beatrix was one of the eleven founding members of the American Society of Landscape Architects (ASLA), which marked a coming of age of the landscape design profession. Beatrix was a frequent visitor at The Mount. She spent the summer there in 1903 when the formal gardens were being laid out, and she certainly gave advice.[48]

Beyond the kitchen garden and the stable, the road curved into the dense woods for about 400 yards before culminating in an opening and a broad lawn that led to the walls of the forecourt of the house. The allée and woodland drive were French in feeling, juxtaposed with the lawn, which was an American element. The rock outcroppings to the north of the house and elsewhere were retained as part of the landscape.

Edith spent considerable time in the woods surrounding the house creating paths and transplanting ferns. This area might be called the "wild garden" and stood in contrast to the elaborate French-inspired entry or the Italian gardens to the east. Some of Edith's inspiration came from various landscape books in her library, which ranged from Andrew Jackson Downing's classic *A Treatise on the Theory and Practice of Landscape Gardening*

(sixth edition, 1859) to William Robinson's *The Wild Garden* (third edition, 1883), inscribed "Edith Wharton 1888." There were many more books on landscape and gardens, which demonstrate the range of her interests.[49] For the "wild garden" Edith called upon the assistance of George B. Dorr, a noted conservationist who founded Arcadia National Park in Maine and wrote extensively on gardens. Dorr came from an elite Boston background and became a friend of the Whartons. Thanking him for his help with wild, or native plant species, she wrote: "We have been off in the motor digging ferns for our rocky slopes, and now I have discovered a stony pasture near Great Barrington full of the 'sweet fern' which is so rarely found in this region, and I'm going to fetch a load of it tomorrow."[50] The result was a series of informal winding paths and rock gardens around the house and through the estate, where Edith and her guests could meander and enjoy nature.

The Terrace and Gardens

The terrace and staircase are supported by a rubblestone base.

The terrace that opened off the main floor allowed for a vantage point to see the gardens below. Twenty-five feet wide outside the drawing room, the terrace offered an ideal place for entertainment and lounging with a spectacular view of the gardens and Laurel Lake beyond. Integral to the design was Edith's research and writing of *Italian Villas and Their Gardens* (1904). The concept of a terrace off the main rooms delineated by balustrades, the views, and the generous terrace steps had sources in the Villa Gamberaia, the Villa Chigi, and the Villa Campi, which were all illustrated in the book. Edith had previously written on Italian gardens in a variety of travel pieces and stories, such as one published in *Scribner's* in August 1900. She wrote to Codman from Lenox, where she was summering: "See how you like my description of a Palladian villa, & whether you don't think that Maxfield Parrish's illustrations are delightful."[51] Parrish's photographic magical realist illustrations fit well with Edith's descriptions of Veneto palaces, villas, and gardens planned in "all manner of agreeable surprises in the way of water-jets that drenched you unexpectedly, and hermits in caves, and wild men that jumped at you out of thickets."[52] *Italian Villas and Their Gardens* was commissioned in 1903 as a series of articles for the *Century Magazine* and then collected as a book. Illustrations consisted of color renderings by Parrish, photographs that Edith collected, and a few drawings. She dedicated the book to Vernon Lee, who had provided her with access to some of the villas and gardens, and as Edith wrote: "who, better than any one else, has understood and interpreted the garden-magic of Italy."[53] A natural successor to *The Decoration of Houses*, *Italian Villas and Their Gardens* contained many of the same themes; principles could be extracted from the gardens abroad and applied at home. The book is not about horticulture—"The Italian garden does not exist for its flowers, its flowers exist for

GAMBERAIA

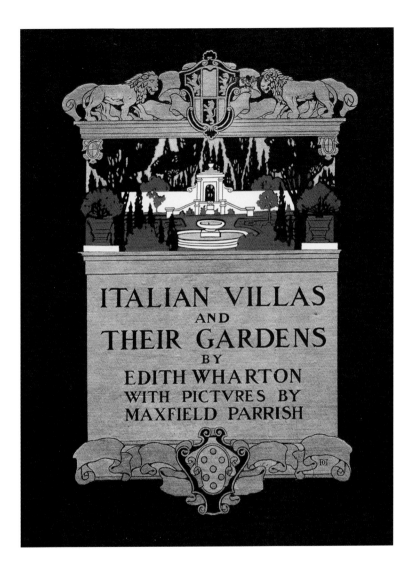

Cover and illustration of the Villa Gamberaia from Italian Villas and Their Gardens*.*

Overleaf: Staircase from the terrace to the gardens.

it"—but a treatment of gardens as architectural assemblages. As Edith observed, "Never perhaps have natural advantages been utilized with so little perceptible straining after effect, yet with so complete a sense of the needful adjustment between landscape and architecture."[54] Charles Adams Platt had written two brief articles in 1893, which were collected as a short book entitled *Italian Gardens* the following year.[55] Interestingly, Edith never mentioned Platt's work. Her book was longer, more comprehensive, and knowledgeable; it helped to fuel the rage for Italian gardens in America and led her to her own creation at The Mount.

Her description of the Villa Gamberaia near Settigano could almost be what

she created in Lenox: "The plan of the Gamberaia . . . combines . . . almost every typical excellence of the old Italian garden: free circulation of sunlight and air about the house; abundance of water; easy access to dense shade; sheltered walks with different points of view; variety of effect produced by the skillful use of different levels; and finally breadth and simplicity of composition."[56]

For the terrace at The Mount, Hoppin designed a staircase reminiscent of the one shown in Campbell's elevation of Belton House (never built) and also that at the Villa Gamberaia illustrated by Parrish in *Italian Villas*. A small niche with a lion's head fountain in the center of the lower landing became a favorite setting for photographs.

Lion's head fountain and balustrade

Grass steps lead from
the northeast corner of
the house toward the
Flower Garden.

View of the Lime Walk from the Flower Garden.

Lime Walk and Gardens

Below the staircase two more grass terraces were graded, and a walk of crushed marble linking two main gardens was added between 1903 and 1905. The 300-foot-long cross-axial walk, known as the "Lime Walk," was planted with a clipped hemlock hedge and a double row of lindens. On the north was a flower garden with a rectangular pool with a dolphin fountain, designed in 1903. Laid out in 1905 on the southern axis was a sunken stone-walled garden with a circular pool. Edith's diary for late October 1905 records "F. Hoppin came about garden" next to the entry "H. of M. best-selling book in New York."[57] Hoppin drew up the plan for the southern

*Above: View from the
Flower Garden to the
meadow.*

*Left: View of the
Flower Garden from
the terrace.*

Above: Trellis niche designed by Codman for Land's End reinstalled at The Mount.

Overleaf: View of the Flower Garden and niche from the Lime Walk.

Opposite: Trellis niche recreated and reinstalled in the Flower Garden.

The walled garden is now covered with climbing hydrangea and Virginia creeper.

Overleaf: The Walled Garden.

Second overleaf: The Lime Walk leads to a series of terraces and steps descending to the Walled Garden.

garden in consultation with Edith. The trellis niche Codman had designed for Land's End was the focal point of the Flower Garden while statues stood in niches in the Walled Garden. A pergola projected from the Walled Garden toward the meadow.

The meadow opening below the gardens tied the formal landscaping around the house to the middle distance of natural forest and the lake. Paths cut in the woods and meadow led to Laurel Lake, whose sparkling glint made a transition to the far distance of the Berkshire Hills. As a visitor to The Mount recorded: "Looking down upon these two gardens, separated from each other by the terraced lawns, as you stand on the broad veranda of the villa, the glory of their coloring actually vibrates in the sunlight; yet framed as they are in spacious green, they do not clash with the distant prospect."[58]

CHAPTER 3

Life at The Mount

inalmente!" Edith wrote to Sally Norton at the end of September 1902; she and Teddy had moved into The Mount.[1] *Lenox Life* reported a housewarming party with Egerton Winthrop, Reginald Vanderbilt, and the Sloanes among those in attendance. The speed with which the house was built and economies in the construction created problems that would constantly reappear, but at least Edith now resided in a house that represented her tastes and where she hoped she could pursue a life filled with writing, friends, and an adoring husband. Part of the goal would be realized, and part not. No longer would the memory of her mother be present as it had been in Newport, but she now had Teddy's mother and his "dull" brothers, sisters, and sisters-in-law to contend with.[2] Lenox, she believed, would be different from the "flat frivolity," the "trivialities," the "depressing climate . . . and the vapid watering-place amusements" of Newport, which she had scathingly portrayed in "The Line of Least Resistance" and in "The Twilight of the Gods."[3]

Lenox and the Berkshires

Lenox in 1900 seemed to offer an antidote to Newport, even though it had the sobriquet of "inland Newport." Surrounded by forested mountains and graced with several lakes, the town appeared to be a bucolic setting. But, as Edith discovered, the Berkshires contained many different layers and levels of society.

Edith Wharton, c. 1903.

Lenox and Stockbridge—which lay a few miles to the south—were two of the prime summer resort areas that began to emerge in the period after the Civil War. Both had small industries, such as the Lenox Iron Works, which lay just outside of the village. North by about twenty miles lay the towns of Pittsfield, Adams, and North Adams, filled with large factories for shoes, cotton, wool, and electronics, and thousands of workers. To the south of Stockbridge sat Great Barrington, site of the home of Mrs. Mark Hopkins, the widow of one of America's wealthiest individuals with money from the California gold fields and railroads, but also a manufacturing center. Flowing through the valley was the Housatonic River, which supplied power for the major paper mills at nearby Lee and Dalton. On various motoring trips, Edith observed aspects of this industrial landscape that would appear in some of her stories and especially in *The Fruit of the Tree* (1907), which deals with textile mills and the unsuccessful attempts to mitigate the atrocious working and living conditions.

In addition to the bucolic woods of The Mount and Lenox and the harsh industrial landscape was another country of rural poverty, of farm families caught in isolation on the top of hills or in hidden valleys. Many years later Edith wrote: "In those days the snow-bound villages of Western Massachusetts were still grim places, morally and physically: insanity, incest and slow mental and moral starvation were hidden away behind the paintless wooden house-fronts of the long village street, or in the isolated farm-houses on the neighbouring hills; and Emily Bronte would have found as savage tragedies in our remoter valleys as on her Yorkshire moors."[4] These settings and the inhabitants appeared in several of her writings, most notably *Ethan Frome* (1911) and *Summer* (1917).

The Berkshires also offered the inducement of an intellectual and literary life, and some locals dubbed it "the Lake District" in obvious allusion to the literary retreat in northwest England populated by William Wordsworth, Samuel Taylor Coleridge, Robert Southey, and later John Ruskin. Beginning in the 1840s and 1850s, major American authors, such as Nathaniel Hawthorne, Herman Melville, Oliver Wendell Holmes, William Cullen Bryant, and Henry Wadsworth Longfellow, spent time in the Berkshires. The colonial ancestral home of Longfellow's wife was in Pittsfield, and it inspired one of his best-known poems, "The Old Clock on the Stairs" (1845–46), which made a major impact upon American interior decoration, with tall case clocks appearing on stair landings across the country.[5]

In Stockbridge, Catherine Maria Sedgwick ran an impressive salon that attracted many of these literary figures, as well as Harriet Martineau, the actress Fanny Kemble and the painters Thomas Cole and Frederic Edwin Church. Sedgwick's *A New England Tale* (1822), *Hope Leslie* (1827), and *Clarence* (1849), which contained a title-page illustration of a waterfall by George Inness, extolled the beauties and history of the Berkshires. Sedgwick also played a role in the formation of the Laurel Hill Association, the first village improvement society that

Shadow Brook, Henry Neil Wilson, 1893.

aimed to beautify the streetscape of small towns. In a tourist guide of 1902, Raymond DeWitt Mallary, minister at the Church on the Hill in Lenox, noted not only Catherine Sedgwick but also mentioned: "Lately another woman distinguished in letters, Mrs. Edith Wharton, has become enamored of the Berkshire County and is . . . creating here a country seat, beautifully located near Laurel Lake."[6]

The "literary associations," the Lenox minister noted, continued well after the Civil War, when a later generation of the Boston intelligentsia settled in the Berkshire Hills during the summer months.[7] Charles Eliot Norton of Harvard, the first professor of art history at any American college and a friend of Edith's, had a house in Ashfield in the Deerfield Valley. His daughter Sara, or Sally, became a close friend of Edith's with much correspondence between them. Edith's story of 1901 "The

131

Angel at the Grave" certainly reflected Sally Norton's devotion to her father. Richard Watson Gilder, Edith's editor at the *Century*, had a house at Tyringham, and Frank Crowninshield, editor of *Vanity Fair*, spent the summers at Stockbridge. Other summer residents of the area included the sculptors Daniel Chester French and Thomas Shields Clarke, and the authors Owen Wister and I. N. P. Stokes.

Countermanding the Berkshires's intellectual and literary side was the growth beginning in the 1870s of a summer resort for the wealthy, and large "cottages" went up.[8] One of Charles Follen McKim's earliest cottages (while in partnership with William R. Mead and William Bigelow) was for the very wealthy Boston banker Samuel Gray Ward. Located on a hillside overlooking the Tanglewood Bowl, the Ward house (1877–78) attracted much attention in the architectural press, with one writer commenting "that but for a few Queen Anne Fantasies it might pass for an old Puritan's homestead."[9] McKim and his partners (with Stanford White replacing Bigelow after September 1879) went on to design a variety of buildings in the area, including a house near downtown Lenox (1883) for his future wife, Julia Appleton, and her sister and multiple commissions in Stockbridge: St. Paul's Episcopal Church (1885), Naumkeag for Joseph H. Choate (1884–87), and the Casino (1888). A few miles south in Great Barrington, the enormous French chateauesque house for Mrs. Mark Hopkins, subsequently known as Searles Castle (1884–86), introduced a whole new scale to the Berkshires.

Elm Court, Peabody & Stearns, 1886.

The status-seeking ante continued to rise with fancy houses and country estates springing up throughout the Berkshires. Henry James, on one of his visits to The Mount, noted the "injury" inflicted by the "summer people" to the Berkshires, which he felt contained the "heart of New England which makes so pretty a phrase for print and so stern a fact, as yet, for feeling."[10] Large estates were formed, such as Folly Farm in Great Barrington owned by Frederick Pearson, an electrical engineer and businessman who accumulated thirteen thousand acres. William Whitney, a lawyer, street railway magnate, and politician, purchased many farms in the Lenox and Lee area to create a game preserve of eleven thousand acres.[11] Next door to The Mount was Erskine Park, the estate of George Westinghouse, the electric king, who built a vast house with a power plant. A frieze of 1,500 lightbulbs decorated the house, and he produced enough power to light the streets of Lenox, as well as Edith's house.

Bellefontaine, Carrère & Hastings, 1898.

Although *The Decoration of Houses* warned against electric light "with its harsh white glare," which made the salon "look like a railway-station," Edith did allow some "modern improvements."[12] In Lenox twenty-six big houses were constructed in the 1880s, and by 1902 another forty-two had been completed.[13] A large hotel, the Curtis House, dominated the downtown, surrounded by small shops that served the summer community.

Lenox began to resemble Newport. Anson Phelps Stokes, a manufacturer and banker, built Shadow Brook in 1893, reputedly the largest country house in America after G. W. Vanderbilt's Biltmore in North Carolina. When the Whartons arrived, Bellefontaine, designed for Giraud Foster by Carrère & Hastings, had just been completed at a cost reportedly in excess of $1 million. Elm Court by Peabody & Stearns for William Douglas and Emily Vanderbilt Sloane was a gigantic "cottage" that rambled for over a hundred yards along a mountainside.

Although the residents of Lenox and the nearby towns rejected the Newport allusion, many commonalities existed. As a writer for *Lenox Life* observed in 1901: "Newport is known as the greatest watering place and 'resort' in America; Lenox has never aspired to that position." Instead of giant mansions Lenox had "many beautiful country houses . . . but not 'show' places." Newport's life was "fast" but Lenox avoided that "with the possible exception of a little 'bridge' now and then." A visit to both places at the height of the season would show "more conclusively that anything else why the better classes of New York society, and people of more conservative tastes prefer life in the Berkshires to life at Newport." The writer described the amenities of the area, including golf, long country drives, fishing, boating, and, of course, "dinner parties and the informal dances which are the means of entertaining."[14] Assisting in the attraction of the Berkshires was the ease of access by railroad, in contrast to the steamer from Manhattan to Newport that took at least eight hours. The Berkshire division of the New York, New Haven & Hartford railroad brought New York passengers to Pittsfield in three hours and thirty-seven minutes. Especially important was the summer express train, which left Grand Central at 3:30 PM and arrived at the Lenox station at 7:27 PM. And on Sundays a special train left Lenox at 6:27 PM, "much appreciated by the young business men and others."[15]

Running The Mount

The household staff at The Mount resembled those of other large and elite houses of the period. Divisions between the males and females were strict, and in general the maids remained behind the scenes, seldom to be seen or heard. Edith's devotion to some of the help does stand out; many would stay with her for decades on different continents. Daniel Berkeley Updike, the designer of *The Decoration of Houses*, recalled both Edith and Teddy showing "real consideration too for the servants and those employed on the place." He told Edith that she was the "most considerate person to your servants," and she replied, "Perhaps that is because I was brought up in a household where there was no consideration for them at all."[16]

Catherine Gross.

The names and identities of all the staff at The Mount are not known. Quarters were provided for approximately twenty individuals. About eight staff lived in the main house, the females along with the butler and cook/chef. Running of the house was divided between the housekeeper, Catherine Gross, and the head butler, Alfred White. It is doubtful that all the maids' quarters in the attic were occupied, and some of the rooms may have been used by servants accompanying guests. Similarly it remains unclear whether all the quarters in the stable were ever occupied. Finally, the farm hands lived in the farmhouse.

Edith's relationship with the help can be seen in several instances where records remain. Catherine Gross, nicknamed "Grossie" by Edith, came to work for her in October 1884, a few months prior to her marriage. Born in the Alsace region, Grossie grew up in straighted circumstances and bore an illegitimate son when she was seventeen. She then immigrated to New York and would remain with Edith for the remainder of her life, until her death at age 81 in 1933 in France. They were devoted to each other and celebrated every year the anniversary of her being hired. In time Catherine graduated from serving as Edith's personal maid to the role of housekeeper.[17] Photographs depict a stout woman holding several of the Wharton's dogs. And Edith's short story "The Lady's Maid's Bell" (1902) certainly depicts Grossie.

Alfred White originally went to work as a young man for Teddy as his valet in 1884. Although he continued to serve Teddy, he rose to be the head butler at Land's End and then at The Mount. His allegiance lay with Edith, and after the divorce in 1913 he remained with her, receiving a generous bequest at her death. Gaillard Lapsley remembered: "White was the only one . . . who stood on an equal moral footing with her. . . he always treated her with a frank though respectful severity which so far from resenting she relied upon."[18]

William Parlett, right, and his family at Land's End.

The Whartons' coachman, William Parlett, and his wife emigrated from England to the United States in 1895, and by 1897 they were employed at Land's End. They followed the Whartons to Lenox and lived there with their growing family of a son and two daughters upstairs in the stable. Edith admired Parlett, and in a 1908 letter she called him "a savant ornithologist," for having heard a cuckoo.[19]

Charles Cook was hired as the chauffeur when the Whartons purchased their motor car in 1904. Initially he lived in the nearby town of Lee, but he traveled with Edith and Teddy to Europe and drove stoically in Paris, rural France, and Italy. After the divorce, he continued as Edith's chauffeur and even drove her in the war zones during World War I. After he suffered a stroke in 1921, Edith gave him a life pension and he returned to the United States.[20]

The estate superintendent, who also acted as the head gardener, was Thomas Reynolds. The position of gardener was very important, and initially the Whartons hired an incompetent individual who, perhaps suffering from drink, allowed the gardens to dry up from lack of water. He was fired in 1903 and Reynolds hired. He excelled and Edith described him as "my devoted and admirable head gardener."[21] Reynolds and his family occupied the gate lodge but left in 1911 as the Whartons were considering selling the estate.

A most intriguing character is Anna Bahlmann. In 1874, at the age of 24, she began teaching German and acting as a tutor to 12-year-old Edith. During the Jones family's European sojourn in 1879–80, she became very close to Edith, introducing her to museums, galleries, cathedrals, and grand houses. "Tonnie," as Edith addressed her in many letters, eventually became her secretary, typing and editing manuscripts and also handling correspondence. She also helped to run the Whartons' houses when they were abroad, although she travelled extensively on her own. Bahlmann never achieved the same social status as Edith, and for mysterious reasons is only mentioned by name once in *A Backward Glance*. Tonnie came to The Mount to assist during Edith's writing periods, but except for a few nights she did not stay in the house. "The boarding houses are not better than last year," Edith warned, so Bahlmann would stay at the Curtis Hotel with the Whartons paying the bill. Until her death in 1916, Bahlmann played a central role in Edith's career and without her, some of the writings might not exist.[22]

Remaining unknown are the other individuals who cooked and served the meals, washed the dishes and laundry, kept the furnace going, cleaned and repaired the house, worked in the gardens, fed the horses, and mowed the hay. They are the silent backdrop, the ghosts or angels who appear at times in Edith's stories.

Elevator and pantry.

Life at The Mount

The Mount was Edith's most complete realization of a total environment. Here she presided. Instead of the ocean, the Berkshires offered the mountains and varieties of scenery that Edith genuinely liked better, for as she wrote, "I was to know the joys of six or seven months a year among fields and woods of my own, and . . . the deep joy of communion with the earth."[23] Henry James, who came to visit several times, wrote: "It is an exquisite and marvelous place, a delicate French chateau mirrored in a Massachusetts pond (repeat not this formula), and a monument to the almost too impeccable taste of its so accomplished mistress. Every comfort prevails."[24]

The Whartons occupied The Mount for six to seven months of the year, usually from June to Thanksgiving and occasionally Christmas, between 1902 and late 1907. The remainder of the year they traveled in Italy, France, and England. Unfortunately Teddy's mental and physical health continued to decline with even more speed after 1902, and changes of scene were needed. Edith's last visit to The Mount came in the summer of 1911.

Typically Edith awoke about 6 AM and spent the morning in bed writing letters and composing her novels, stories, and articles. She dropped the pages on the floor for Anna Bahlmann to collect and type up for review. On her bed frequently were one or two dogs. Edith would also plan the day's activities. Percy Lubbock recalled: "In those early morning hours of Edith's seclusion over her story . . . a gay little note, thrown off as it were between chapters, would appear for the guest on his breakfast

Trinity Episcopal Church, Lenox.

tray, with a greeting and a plan for the day."[25] At 11 AM Edith descended the stairs and the day's activities would start. She would inspect the gardens with any guests in residence, then lunch, and the afternoon might be horseback or buggy riding, and visits to town or other locations. After the Whartons acquired a car, the early morning writing might be curtailed so that the group could set out on a long journey to visit friends, such as the Nortons some eighty miles away, or explore the mills and little villages of the Berkshires. Back at The Mount, the evening would focus around the predinner gathering, the meal, and then conversations that could last until late at night in the library or drawing room. Frequently Teddy retired to bed first, since he had little interest in the literary and artistic topics.

Edith took an active interest in the gardening and directed her nurseryman Thomas Reynolds and staff about plantings. She loved her gardens and wrote to Sally Norton about the "mass of bloom" and her ten varieties of phlox, snapdragons, and lilacs, and the profusion of pinks, blues, purples, and whites.[26] She entered flowers in the local competitions sponsored by the Lenox Horticultural Society, and in 1904 she received one first prize, five second prizes, and three third prizes; the next year she received seven first prizes.[27]

Summer pleasures in
the Berkshires included
afternoons by the pond,
luncheon under the
trees, and croquet
matches. Edith
Wharton was
photographed
smoking on a picnic.

Edith volunteered at the Lenox Library, where she joined the board in 1902. In addition to annual contributions, she helped organize its catalogue.[28] A library very similar in style appears in *Summer*: Charity Royall walks "down a brick path to a queer little brick temple with white wooden columns supporting a pediment." A young man, Lucius Harney, enters looking for "'books on the old houses about here. I suppose, for that matter, this part of the country hasn't been much explored. They all go on doing Plymouth and Salem. So stupid.'" He then explains: "'I'm an architect, you see, and I'm hunting up old houses in these parts.'"[29]

Edith also participated in other local organizations such as the Village Improvement Society, but she found them wearing; she wrote to Sally Norton in 1904, "I am so tied with Library meetings, Village Committees & Flower Show Committees."[30]

Teddy's daily activities included running the stable and farm, and he took some interest in the gardening. Taking either a buggy or a car, he would run household errands, driving up to Pittsfield or down to Lee. During the fall he hunted. He played golf frequently at the Lenox Club, where he served on the board and also tried to get local taxes reduced, claiming "excessive taxation."[31] In 1903 the Whartons discovered the game of Ping-Pong. Edith complained that August was very cold and that "fires every evening & violent games of Ping-Pong alone keep us from sinking into an arctic slumber."[32]

The Whartons intermittently attended services at Trinity Episcopal Church, which stood across the street from Teddy's mother's house. The church was where "nearly all the [summer] cottagers worship." It had a mixed history in that McKim had submitted a design in 1888, but Colonel. Richard T. Auchmuty, one of the leading summer residents and an "old-school gentlemen of New York polite society," took over the plans.[33] Colonel Auchmuty (he served on General Meade's staff during the Civil War) and his wife, the former Ellen Schermerhorn, were the leading donors for the new church building. Auchmuty shifted some of McKim's elements around, compromising the integrity of the design of the Romanesque-style building. Edith knew the rector Harold Arrowsmith, who served between 1896 and 1909. One of the most striking incidents in Edith's Berkshire tales involves a funeral in a small hilltop village. She relates the source: "I may mention that every detail about the colony of drunken mountain outlaws described in "Summer" was given to me by the rector of the church at Lenox (near which we lived), and that the lonely peak I have called "the Mountain" was in reality Bear Mountain, an isolated summit not more than twelve miles from our own home. The rector had been fetched there by one of the mountain outlaws to read the Burial Service over a woman of evil reputation; and when he arrived everyone in the house of mourning was drunk, and the service was performed as I have related it."[34]

The stable was an important focus of the activities of a country place. Different

Lenox Horse Show.

horses were required for riding and for drawing carriages. The Mount's stables housed several surreys and buggies of different sizes, along with the horses whose names were Duchess, Dowager, Don, and Dobbins. It is likely that Edith chose them, since she delighted in naming things. Gaillard Lapsley recalled Edith on a brilliant summer day in Lenox when they went to the post office to send a telegram: "I saw her in the trim two-seated open carriage with a light fringed cover like an old fashioned pony phaeton, her coachman in front and a pair of smart cobs."[35] Also in the stable were riding horses, and Edith's mounts were Fatty and Frank.[36] Teddy had several horses, including one named Countess. The Whartons entered the local horse show in 1901 and 1902, and Teddy received fourth place in several classes.[37] They attended the 1904 show, but they did not compete, perhaps because of Teddy's increasing bouts of depression. Teddy delighted in escorting guests in his Mineola cart while Edith guided others on horseback through the woodlands. The horses remained at The Mount, but they were being replaced by motoring, a new activity that came to dominate American life.

In 1900, prior to the Whartons' purchase of The Mount property, the local newspaper reported: "The automobile is to furnish a new element in Lenox life this season, and many of the cottages who have already fallen victims to this fascinating sport in town, will not only bring one automobile here, but three or four . . . There

143

Edith Wharton mounted on Fatty.

are a number of expert women motorists in Newport, and there seems to be no reason why Lenox should not follow the example already set."[38] For the next several years, the paper was filled with articles on motor cars and the new possibilities of travel. While in Europe during the winter of 1904, the Whartons purchased an automobile for touring, but they decided not to bring it back to the States. Instead Teddy purchased a Pope-Hartford car from the local Lenox dealer. With a ten horsepower motor and a removable tonneau, the car, which Edith nicknamed "George" (after George Sand the writer), could comfortably seat four or five people: the chauffeur Charles Cook and Teddy in front, and in the rear Edith, frequently with a dog in her lap, and guests, such as Henry James. These so-called "motor flights" gave access to a much bigger area, and in a day they could visit friends such as the Nortons over in Ashland and return home. In time they went further afield to Worcester and Beverley, Massachusetts, New Hampshire, Vermont, and even Newport. But the important area was the Berkshires, and here Edith discovered "derelict villages with Georgian churches and balustrade house-fronts, exploring slumberous mountain

valleys and coming back, weary but laded with a new harvest of beauty."[39] Out of this exploring came elements of her novels set in the Berkshires. Many years later Edith recalled a critic claiming that *Ethan Frome* was "an interesting example of a successful New England story written by someone who knew nothing of New England! *Ethan Frome* was written after I had spent ten years in the hill-region where the scene is laid, during which years I had come to know well the aspect, dialect, and mental and moral attitude of the hill-people." She went on to note that "*Summer* deals with the same class and type as those portrayed in *Ethan Frome* and has the same setting, might have sufficed to disprove the legend—but once such a legend is started it echoes on as long as its subject survives."[40]

The automobile trips became legendary, and Henry James delighted in the tours; to his brother William he wrote: "I greatly enjoyed the whole Lenox countryside, seeing it as I did by the aid of the Whartons' big strong commodious new motor . . . if I were rich I shouldn't hesitate to take up with it."[41] Not all of the trips were pleasant, and as Edith wrote: "I remember in particular one summer night

Teddy Wharton on horseback holding Jules.

Charles Cook at the wheel of "George" at the front door of The Mount.

when Henry James, Walter Berry, my husband and I sat by the roadside till near dawn while our chauffeur tried to persuade "George" to carry us back to the Mount."[42]

Charles Cook, the chauffeur, recalled many years later the experience of the Whartons' very first drive, when they did not have a windshield and hence the dust from the road caused a case of laryngitis, with Edith spending several days in bed to recover. Some of Cook's most memorable descriptions involved trying to find directions, especially in England; Henry James had no sense of direction, even in his own town. About James, Cook recalled he spoke "with maddening slowness seeming to weigh every sentence as he uttered it and breasting at times 'a sea of parentheses,'" and his patience under the circumstances "led Mrs. Wharton to dub him 'the mildest of men.'"[43]

Entertainment played an essential role at The Mount and at all the cottages and country houses. The local gossip sheet *Lenox Life* provided instructions for those who needed them about how to handle a house party: "Society people of the present age know how to entertain," but "the Art of entertaining is a difficult one." For the

A "motor flight";
Edith Wharton is
in the back seat.

guests "amusements must be provided," and the host or hostess "will very likely tell his guests what is on the day's schedule . . . This is the English idea of entertaining, and if one wishes to lounge about the house and read an novel instead of playing golf or going driving it is considered perfectly proper and right." The important element was to gather "a party of people who are congenial" and "Here in Lenox few strangers are admitted." The result was "one big happy family."[44] A bit earlier in the summer of 1901, the *Lenox Life* writer extolled the community's virtues: "New ideas and new schemes, not to speak of new people, have appeared recently, but nothing can spoil the spirit of comraderie [sic] which is one of the principal charms of Lenox life during the summer."[45]

The Mount was a scene of constant entertainment when the Whartons were in residence. The arriving guest would be greeted by Edith with a dog in arms at the front door, and as one recalled she "observed the merciful custom of offering her guests champagne after a long railway journey."[46] The list of guests is extensive and includes the several visits of Henry James, Egerton Winthrop, Paul and Minnie Bourget, James Van Alen, Walter Berry, and Daniel Berkeley Updike. In spite of

On the terrace, Walter Berry on the balustrade and a trio of country gentlemen—Henry James, Teddy Wharton, and John Hubbard Sturgis—admiring the view.

Overleaf: View from the terrace to the Walled Garden and woodlands.

*Walter Berry in the
trellis niche in the
Flower Garden.*

the increasingly blustering and sometimes oppressive presence of Teddy, Edith forged new relationships with leading American intellectuals. Through the Nortons she came to know and host Edward Robinson, the director of the Metropolitan Museum of Art. Known as a funny person with a dry sense of humor, Robinson was an expert on classical art. Robert Grant, the author of *Unleavened Bread* (1900), an account of a ruthless fortune-hunting divorcée that Edith greatly admired and that served as a partial model for Edith's *Custom of the Country* (1913), came to stay many times. The illustrators Moncure Robinson, who contributed to some of Edith's early work, and Maxfield Parrish whose colorful renderings appeared in *Italian Villas and Their Gardens*, visited. George "Bay" Cabot Lodge, the son of the Massachusetts senator and a passionate poet, recited his poems during the evenings.

Left: Teddy Wharton.

Above: Daniel Chester French.

These and many more came for a few days or weeks, and participated in the parties, horseback riding, walks, and visits in the auto to various scenic wonders of the area, as well as some not so pretty—the decayed villages. Evenings would be spent on the terrace talking, reading, and stargazing. The wine cellar was well stocked though Edith generally abstained.[47] Henry James on his first visit in 1904 endeared himself to Edith by reading poetry from books in the library: Browning, Arnold, Baudelaire, and Emily Bronte. She described the event:

He read from his soul, and no one who never heard him read poetry knows what that soul was. Another day someone spoke of Whitman, and it was a joy to me to discover that James thought him, as I did, the greatest of American poets. "Leaves of Grass" was put into his hands, and all that evening we sat rapt while he wandered from "The Song of Myself" to "When lilacs last in the door-yard bloomed" (when he read "Lovely and soothing Death" his voice filled the hushed room like an organ adagio), and thence let himself be lured on to the mysterious music of "Out of the Cradle," reading, or rather crooning it in a mood of subdued ecstasy till the fivefold invocation to Death tolled out like the knocks in the opening bars of the Fifth Symphony.[48]

As Percy Lubbock observed, "Nobody could deny that to be a guest in a house of Mrs. Wharton was a deeply, deliciously delicately luxurious experience."[49]

Social life extended beyond houseguests to include the Berkshire resort society as well. Edith could be dismissive of that group, and although many of Wharton's biographers claimed she was at odds, she still entertained many of the locals.[50] Edith could make caustic remarks, such as when one wealthy lady showed off her house and said: "And I call this my Louis Quinze room," Edith supposedly retorted, "Why, my dear?"[51] Certainly Edith disdained the nouveaux riches in general, but she entertained many of the locals, such as Joseph Hodges Choate of Naumkeag, Charlotte Barnes of nearby Coldbrooke, the Girand Fosters of Bellefontaine, and redheaded Ethel Cram of Highwood (the site of the present Tanglewood Music festival), an accomplished pianist who died in a tragic horse-automobile accident in 1905. Her death appears in *The Fruit of the Tree*.

Daniel Chester French and his wife, Mary, were frequent visitors to The Mount. Chesterwood, French's house and studio designed by Henry Bacon, later architect of the Lincoln Memorial in Washington, D.C., was just outside Stockbridge. He was the foremost American sculptor of the time. The Whartons and the Frenches visited back and forth, and Mary French later recorded that Edith "came to see . . . each new development in our little place, . . . and brought her friends to see it—among others, Mr. Henry James whom Mr. French had known years before in London."[52] French wrote a letter to Edith about *The House of Mirth*: "I know of no more clear-cut, living, breathing, vital human creature in fiction than Miss Bart— I should not think of even speaking of her by her first name!—who is as real to me as if I had actually known her. How could you bear to bring her beautiful, arrogant head so low when you know how noble a woman she might have become if you had but given her a chance!"[53]

Edith Wharton, c. 1920.

CHAPTER 4

Afterward

he Whartons' involvement with The Mount diminished significantly in late 1907, and Teddy sold the property without Edith's permission during September 1911. Her last view of the house and gardens came shortly prior to sailing to Europe in September, and she never returned. Twenty-three years later she explained: "I was too happy there ever to want to revisit it as a stranger."[1]

There were a number of reasons for giving up The Mount. First, Teddy's melancholia, or mental instability, grew increasing unmanageable. As early as 1902 he suffered a breakdown, and as Ogden Codman delightedly reported: "Teddy Wharton seems to be losing his mind which makes it very hard for his wife . . . he has been queer for a long time getting slowly worse." Codman wrote his mother that Teddy had gone to Hoppin's office "so enraged that he 'foamed' at the mouth."[2] Though his instability went into remission at times, it returned periodically, and by 1907 his nervous collapse became overwhelming. He did not want to stay in Lenox, and consequently they traveled, frequently separately, with Teddy spending time in various sanatoriums and spas ranging from Arkansas and Indiana to Switzerland. Not engaged in his wife's literary life but dependent on her for financial support, he could be maniacal. In addition alcohol added to the problem, and he had at least one affair.[3]

Edith, while still devoted to The Mount, suffered her own crisis, which began in October 1907 when Morton Fullerton came to visit. She had met Fullerton the previous April in Paris, and they struck up a friendship that blossomed into something more. Fullerton, who grew up in Massachusetts and attended Phillips Andover

Edith Wharton on the terrace at Ste. Claire.

Academy and then Harvard College, had been a student of Charles Eliot Norton and was one of Henry James's most promising literary protégés. By the early twentieth century, he resided in Paris, where he wrote articles for various periodicals, including the London *Times*, and attempted to write a book. He was well known and fêted in literary circles. Oscar Wilde, when he came to Paris after his prison sentence in 1898, contacted Fullerton, who had had an affair with Lord Ronald Gower, the model for the decadent hero of *The Picture of Dorian Gray*. Extremely good looking and charming, Fullerton was bisexual and had a series of affairs with women and men that stretched over many years. Henry James wrote to Fullerton concerning his proposed trip to the United States in 1907: "Let Mrs. Wharton know of your American presence and whereabouts that she may ask you to come to her at Lenox—as she earnestly desires to do."[4] The visit went well. They walked the estate and drove around the Berkshires, and Edith experienced "the old woman's bloom" and began writing a secret journal for Fullerton.[5] After Fullerton left, she advanced her sailing date to France from January to December 5.[6] In Paris, although Fullerton already had a mistress to whom he was secretly engaged, he was somewhat untangled by April, and the relationship with Edith took the final turn into a full-blown affair.

While Fullerton and Teddy were partial causes of Edith's removal from The Mount, she also found herself increasingly estranged from America. Her quandary has been noted, but it grew, especially with some of the reaction to *The House of Mirth*. In 1911 according to the New York gossip sheet *Town Topics*, the Whartons were selling the Mount because although "feted by the rich in their country homes," *The House of Mirth* had caused an uproar: "Lenox residents damned the book . . . There followed a social blight . . . and finally the Whartons quit the game and went abroad."[7] Edith wrote to Bernard Berenson at nearly the same time: "Really, the amenities, the sylvan sweetness, of the Mount (which you would have to see to believe) reconcile me to America, and then she signed it: "The Hermit of Western Massachusetts, Edith Wharton."[8]

Although Edith and Teddy came for a short visit in 1908, they lived abroad during 1909 and 1910, renting The Mount to Alfred and Mary Shattuck. Teddy did visit briefly in 1909 since he was ostensibly in charge of both The Mount and Edith's finances. She, of course, continued to write during these years—*Ethan Frome* appeared in 1911 and *Custom of the Country*, which suffered many interruptions, finally appeared in 1913. Meanwhile Teddy's condition continued to deteriorate, and at the same time he speculated with Edith's money, which he lost, along with embezzling some. Edith and Teddy stayed together nominally, and in July 1911 they returned to The Mount, where Edith presided over her last gathering. Henry James, Gaillard Lapsley, and John Hugh Smith came as guests. A few days later Teddy arrived, and a scene of "violent & unjustified abuse" took place. James left hurriedly and wrote to Edith: "2 things surely emerge clear: 1st that it is vital to get rid of the

Pavilion Colombe,
St.-Brice-sous-Fôret.

absolutely unworkable burdens & complications of the Mount; & 2nd that with the recurrent scenes of violence you must insist on saving your life by a separate existence . . . settle the Mount question first, & the rest will offer itself in much simpler form."[9] Edith and Teddy attempted to reconcile. Edith offered to allow Teddy to stay and run The Mount, but things again broke down with arguments and violent rantings. Word had gotten out that the estate was for sale, and an offer was made but then rejected. Negotiations took place in August with various purchasers; one offer was declined on September 2, possibly Edith's last day at The Mount. She decided to return to Europe for a rest cure, sailing on September 7, 1911, and gave Teddy the power of attorney to complete the sale but only with her approval.[10]

Right after Edith departed, Teddy and the Lenox real estate agent William D. Curtis met with the Shattucks, who had rented the property in 1909–10, and by September 11, he sold the estate, including the house, its contents, and the farm, for $180,000. Indicating that some of the Whartons' problems were public knowledge, the *Berkshire Evening Eagle* reported it was "no surprise in Lenox to those who have been kept informed as to the trend of events with regard to the sale." And then it noted that "The Mount cost Mr. and Mrs. Wharton close to $250,000, and the purchase price was not far from $180,000."[11]

Gaillard Lapsley.

Edith landed in France and discovered Teddy's actions. She wrote to Morton Fullerton: "Yes—he promised not to sell the Mount to any one, at any price, till after I had reached Paris . . . Yet when I landed I found his cable say he had sold!"[12] It was "an awful wrench" for Edith, and though she tried to put it behind her, it took her several weeks to finally sign the agreement. Teddy would visit her in France several more times, but the marriage was over. On April 15, 1913, the French Tribunal de Grande Instance de Paris granted Edith a divorce from Teddy. The stated reason was his adultery in Boston, London, and France. She obtained the divorce in Paris in an attempt to avoid publicity. She also obtained the right to keep the last name, and henceforth her legal name would be Edith Newbold Wharton.[13] A few months after signing the final deed transfer in Paris, Edith wrote to her close friend Gaillard Lapsley, who was visiting family in Stockbridge: "Write me soon, dear Gaillard. But don't tell anything about the Mount, for there's a great ache there still."[14]

The Mount's Later Owners

The deed to The Mount was transferred to Mary and Albert Shattuck in January 1912, and they and their heirs owned it until 1938. Albert R. Shattuck was a New York banker; his father, a New Orleans banker, had a house in Lenox known as Brookdale, designed by James Renwick, which burned in 1908. The replacement house on the site, built by Newbold Morris, was designed by Hoppin & Koen. Shattuck's wife was the daughter of a New York dry goods merchant who also served as mayor of New York from 1895 to 1897. The Shattucks were very prominent both in New York and Lenox society, and, after the destruction of their Lenox house, they rented The Mount and subsequently purchased it. They renamed it "White Lodge," since the original name was too closely associated with the Whartons. Considerable sums were spent on the grounds and the house over the years, adding reportedly a swimming pool and tennis courts. According to his obituary, "Mr. Shattuck greatly improved the property with formal gardens and winding drives by doing whatever was needed, regardless of expenses, to make it an ideal gentleman's estate."[15] The most notable event connected with the Shattucks occurred in their Washington Square North home in New York, where their former butler robbed them in two different incidents of more than $80,000 of jewelry, and locked Mr. Shattuck in the

wine cellar. After the Shattucks' deaths, a large auction of the contents of White Lodge, or The Mount, was held in October 1935, and what remained of the Wharton furnishings and art were disposed of at that time. Among the goods sold that probably dated to the Wharton occupancy were "a Louis XV occasional table stamped with the name of Nicolas Petit . . . four Louis XV carved and parceled gilded armchairs . . . a Brussels tapestry of the eighteenth century depicting Narcissus at the fountain, and other items."[16] The house went on the market and remained empty until October 1938, when, deep into the Depression, it finally sold for $25,600.

The owners of The Mount from 1938 to 1942 were Louise and Carr V. Van Anda. Carr V. Van Anda had a distinguished career as a journalist and editor in Ohio, Baltimore, and then New York, where Adolph S. Ochs hired him in 1904 to be the managing editor of the *New York Times*. He won many prizes, though ill-

Details of the east facade and cupola of The Mount.

health forced him to begin to step down in 1925; he did not formally relinquish his title until 1932. The Van Andas probably intended to spend all year at the house, but they found the furnace inadequate and only spent the summer months. They made some interior alterations, moving the kitchen from the basement to the main floor and painting various rooms different colors. Taxes were a problem, and Van Anda appealed the local tax appraisal of $70,000, since he had purchased the house for much less. He was successful in having his taxes lowered.

In 1942 the property was sold to the Foxhollow School. A private girls' school founded in 1930 by Aileen M. Farrell, Foxhollow was originally located on a former country estate on the Hudson River. In 1939 Farrell moved the school into Erskine Park, the former Westinghouse estate then known as Holmwood, which abutted The Mount to the south. Foxhollow flourished and grew, and in 1942 Ms. Farrell purchased the 155 acres and buildings of The Mount for $18,000 and the remaining contents of the house for $5,659. Students and faculty moved into The Mount and Ms. Farrell lived in Teddy's former den. Edith's former library served as a study hall/meeting space, the drawing room with a piano was for entertainment, and the senior students had dinner every Sunday in the dining room. Headmistress Farrell explained: "The students will still be trained to help in the upkeep of the grounds and care of the house, and definite courses of cooking, sewing, typewriting and shorthand will be added as a complement to the college preparatory courses."[17] Part of the school's curriculum included horseback riding, and hence The Mount's stables were important and also served as a studio for students. At the main house exterior fire stairs were added and parts of the interior were altered, dividers installed, and while some maintenance was carried out, the impact of the students living in the house took its toll. The grounds deteriorated, the view shed was lost to new growth, and the gardens almost completely disappeared except for the stone walls. By the late 1960s Foxhollow suffered from economic problems; Ms. Farrell partially retired, and some land was sold. The Mount was closed as part of the school in 1972. Much of the furniture was auctioned off, and then a leaking pipe caused the collapse of the drawing room's ornamented plaster ceiling of fruit and flowers. Outside a portion of the wall of the forecourt gave way. Between 1972 and 1976, the house stood empty except for a few months occupancy by the Lenox Arts Center. The group found it very expensive to heat, and the deterioration continued.

Aileen Farrell retained great interest in The Mount and in promoting the legacy of Edith Wharton. Slighted for many years as a female author focused on wealthy society, Wharton began to regain her reputation in the 1960s with new evaluations of American literature. Farrell, along with assistants Ona Meigs Fowler and later Hilda Mumford, turned her energies into making The Mount a historic property.

The Mount was designated a National Historic Landmark on November 11, 1971. Although there is a long history of preserving historic American buildings that dates back to George Washington's Mount Vernon in the mid-nineteenth century (and indeed Edith had argued for saving colonial Newport houses in the 1890s), a major change came with the passage of the Historic Preservation Act in 1966, which mandated state-supported offices to assess all buildings. Spurred by the wholesale destruction of many downtowns by the so-called urban renewal, an entirely new attitude emerged that valued not just the buildings of the colonial and founding fathers' period, but more recent structures that might be classified as Victorian, Colonial Revival, or even American Renaissance. That The Mount was listed so early as a National Historic Landmark indicates the changing nature of Edith's reputation. In 1975, with the publication of R. W. B. Lewis's classic study *Edith Wharton: A Biography*, she emerged in the top rank of American authors.

About the same time, Farrell set up a Committee for the Restoration of The Mount with a number of prestigious individuals on its board, including, as honorary chair, Walter Muir Whitehill, the legendary historian of Boston and librarian of the Athenaeum. As a National Landmark, The Mount successfully applied for state

and federal funding, but the money was never enough and maintenance problems continued.

Shakespeare & Company became the next occupant of The Mount when it rented the property from developer Donald Altschuler in the summer of 1978. Founded by Tina Packer, who envisioned a summer Shakespeare festival in the Berkshires, the location in the former home of one of America's literary giants seemed a natural fit. Shakespeare & Company cleared out much of the debris that had accumulated and discovered that the house had no functioning electric or septic systems. The company lived in the house and the stables, and a stage was erected where a rose garden had been. The company did open the house to tours and it gained a modest reputation as a tourist destination, but its major purpose was not as the home of Edith Wharton, but as a stage for plays.

Steps to Walled Garden.

In 1979 Edith Wharton Restoration (EWR) was created, headed by Lila W. Berle. A local resident and graduate of Foxhollow, she also served on the board of Shakespeare & Company. Members of the EWR board were Paul Ivory, director of Chesterwood; Stephen V. C. Morris, a distant relative of Edith's; Mrs. Lawrence K. Miller, founder and director of Hancock Shaker Village; and others, including the directors of Shakespeare & Company. Inspired by a presentation by John Frisbee, the National Trust for Historic Preservation's director of Endangered Properties, EWR set out to raise funds for the purchase of the property. A complicated procedure ensued in which the National Trust bought the property from the developer for $290,000 and then resold it to EWR, which paid $100,000 in cash and the balance with proceeds from a mortgage by a local bank.

Since the 1980s much work has been accomplished at The Mount, despite financial issues that were widely publicized. The house and gardens have been slowly restored, and the gardens, in particular, have regained the look of the Whartons' period. In 1992 a comprehensive historic structures report, written by Scott Marshall and John G. Waite Associates, was published, which guided the direction of the house restoration. In 2006 a sizable portion of Wharton's private library, which she had moved to France in 1911, was purchased by The Mount. This extraordinary collection, which includes volumes with Wharton's handwritten notes and inscriptions, is now settled in its original home and continues to fascinate visitors and scholars.

The lack of visual or written documentation of the rooms and original furniture has hindered the historic recreation of the interiors. Nevertheless visitors are able to roam the house much more freely than in a typical museum and can experience the rooms much as Wharton might have in her day. To evoke the character of the public rooms, noted interior designers, including Geoffrey Bradfield, Libby Cameron,Charlotte Moss, Henrietta Spencer-Churchill, Michael Trapp, and Bunny Williams, created installations inspired by the original decoration and guided by the

principles of *The Decoration of Houses*. Painted wall panels have been restored, and faux-painted tapestries inspired by those that originally hung have been installed.

The Mount now welcomes more than thirty thousand visitors annually from the United States and across the globe representing a wide range of ages and ethnicities. The property is now fully established as a year-round cultural venue, hosting lectures, theatrical performances, concerts, poetry readings, and guest talks by scholars and artists from around the country. Programming at The Mount reflects Wharton's core interests in the literary arts, interior design and decoration, garden and landscape design.

The shift from historic house museum to dynamic cultural center focused on literature and language has enabled The Mount to attract new audiences. In addition to national and state support, The Mount has received major funding from various private individuals and foundations, and since 2008 its donor base has steadily increased. Today The Mount garners national and international press and enthusiastic interest from all corners of the globe. The financial picture has vastly improved, and The Mount is moving forward as a vibrant cultural and literary center, a living tribute to its remarkable creator.

East wall of the library with French doors to the terrace.

The Mount and Edith Wharton

Edith lived in France for the remainder of her life, having residences in Paris, at Hyeres, and at St.-Brice-sous-Fôret. The affair with Fullerton gradually diminished, though their friendship would endure. She continued her travels and friendships and writing. During World War I, she became deeply involved in rescue efforts with injured military, for which she was honored and about which she wrote extensively. Trips were made to North Africa and elsewhere. In 1921 her novel *The Age of Innocence* received the Pulitzer Prize for Fiction, the first time the prestigious award recognized a woman.

She returned to the United States only once, to accept an honorary doctorate from Yale University in 1923, again the first ever awarded to a woman. On Long Island she stayed with old friends, Eunice and Walter Maynard, in a house designed by Codman. The house reminded her in its plan of The Mount, as did its French atmosphere. She did not go to Lenox.

170

Architecture and decoration would remain a major feature of her writing and her life. Even sixty years later she could recall the "terror," the "intolerable ugliness" of the "Hudson River Gothic" house of her aunt at Rhinecliff, which became the Willows in *Hudson River Bracketed* (1929).[18] The "scientific analysis" and acute perception fostered by her travels in Italy and shown in *The Decoration of Houses* and her own houses would stand her in good stead in her novels. She knew her architectural history; even among American historians she is outstanding in the 1920s for her recognition of Andrew Jackson Downing or Charles Locke Eastlake, as shown in *Hudson River Bracketed* and *Old New York*. Even at the end of her life she remembered the Pompeian red and the frieze of stenciled lotus leaves taken from Owen Jones's *Grammar of Ornament* in the vestibules of old New York houses.[19]

Foreground and background are themes that run through her writing. About Italy she wrote: "The country is divided, not in *partes tres*, but in two: a foreground and a background." The foreground is that of the guidebook, which must be known to understand the background, which is that of the "dawdler, the dreamer, and the serious student."[20] A problem though existed, as she explained: "The American landscape has no foreground and the American mind no background."[21] The architects and artists of the American Renaissance felt the same, and except for the colonial period, American models of the nineteenth century were poor and not worthy of emulation. This cosmopolitan view, European-oriented critique, was in a sense typically American, especially for those who had seen the riches of the Old World. What did America have to offer? *The Decoration of Houses, Italian Villas and Their Gardens,* and The Mount were attempts to fill this emptiness in both the American landscape and the American mind.

Living in France she attempted to explain that culture could not be predicated upon pragmatism and usefulness. As she observed, "The deeper civilization of a country may . . . be measured by the care she gives to her flower-garden—the corner of her life where the supposedly 'useless' arts and graces flourish." The French, she found, saw art in everything, from the curve of a woman's hatbrim to the droop of curtains and the branches of avenues laid out by Le Nôtre. Puritanism ruined America: art became "something apart from life." For Americans art belonged only in museums.[22] This is the lament of "The Spark" in *Old New York*; men of property were vacuous, empty shells sitting in bookless libraries, who couldn't even understand Walt Whitman. "False Dawn," also in *Old New York*, deals with paintings—in this case Italian primitives—which departed from society's accepted notions of how art should look and were rejected. The stories, while fictional, were based on real incidents that Edith had either experienced or knew about, as in the case of the James Jackson Jarves primitive collection. The background of most Americans was nonexistent and they rejected any foreground.

Plasterwork in the dining room.

Edith disliked the architecture and decoration of her youth, but as she grew older she found it useful. And there is an air of reconciliation to what she had earlier despised; the brown stain and Eastlake gewgaws of her youth populate *The Age of Innocence* and *Old New York*. But, as is clear in both the title and the resolution of *The Age of Innocence*, with Newland Archer's son, Dallas, becoming an architect and working for a firm like McKim, Mead & White or Hoppin & Koen, the high point of American design came around 1900. Dallas Archer is part of the American Renaissance; he is designing a "Lakeside palace" for a young Chicago millionaire and thinks nothing of nipping abroad "to look at some Italian gardens." Newland Archer's library, which in the 1870s had been decorated in the Brown Decades style, has by 1907 been done over by the son with "English mezzotints, Chippendale cabinets, [and] bits of blue-and-white." Sitting incongruously midst this high style was a memory of past innocence, an "old Eastlake writing table."[23]

In Wharton's writing, the descriptive elements of a room's furnishings, along with buildings and architects, and the impact of form, color, and setting, reveal character. She even went further, asserting that "character and scenic detail are in fact one to the novelist who has fully assimilated his material." Ellen Olenska and Undine Spragg, to take characters from two very different novels, *The Age of Innocence* and *The Custom of the Country*, respectively, are revealed through the rooms they inhabit. The discerning observer could understand them from just their rooms and furnishings. Edith's fiction is filled with correspondences between people and the rooms they inhabit, but also they can take on sexual references. In the novelette *New Year's Day*, she observes: "The most perilous coquetry may not be in a woman's way of arranging her dress but in her way of arranging her drawing-room." In this case the subject was one of "those women": the middle-aged, striking though not beautiful, but vivacious woman who lives just on the edge of polite society. She is not *declassée*, but she creates a salon of male admirers of all ages and types. "Those women" attracted men, enchanting them not with naked sex or beauty, but rather, "The difference of atmosphere is felt on the very threshold." Their flowers even grow differently, their "lamps and easy-chairs have found a clever way of coming together."[24] In *The Age of Innocence* Newland Archer experiences sexual arousal when he visits Ellen Olenska's rented house, where the drawing room through "the skillful use of a few properties, [had] been transformed into something intimate, 'foreign,' subtly suggestive of old romantic scenes and sentiments." A stretch of red damask, a delicate little Greek bronze, "bits of wreckage," thin-legged art furniture, and two Jacqueminot roses in a slender vase leave Newland Archer flat-footed, tongue-tied, and desperately in love with the Countess Olenska.[25]

Architecture, decoration, and furniture served a great number of purposes in Edith Wharton's life, as in her fiction. The low state of American culture and hence architecture and the visual arts were a great concern, and she worked hard to create an American Renaissance. Throughout her long and sexless marriage to Teddy Wharton, architecture and decoration acted not just as a diversion, but as erotic surrogates. Her passions and loves were poured into them, at Land's End and The Mount. But also in her travels and her writings, from *The Decoration of Houses* to *Old New York*, architecture and decoration are not simply setting for her characters, but they are characters and a guide to action. Without a knowledge of Edith's architectural enthusiasms, much of her fiction remains mute, only partially understood.

After the divorce, Teddy continued his maniacal ways, living principally in Lenox in his mother's former house, where his sister Nannie dedicated herself to him, and also in New York. He died in New York on February 7, 1928, and his funeral was held at Grace Church, where Edith had been baptized in 1862 and where Newland Archer and May Welland's wedding took place in *The Age of Innocence*. He was buried in Lenox at the Church on the Hill in a plot where his mother and sister lay. Edith wrote to several friends about his death, noting, "It came as a happy release, for the real Teddy went years ago."[26] To another friend, Robert Grant, she wistfully wrote, you will "remember him as a charming companion, & the kindest & most sympathetic of beings."[27]

Edith continued to write fiction and published her memoir, *A Backward Glance*, in 1934. She wrote: "The Mount was my first real home, and though it is nearly twenty years since I last saw it (for I was too happy there ever to want to revisit it as a stranger) its blessed influence still lives with me."[28] Her last short story published after her death, "All Souls," is set in an "old" "Colonial" family house, Whitegates, located on the heights "overlooking the stately windings of the Connecticut River." The owners, when "interest in the 'Colonial' began to revive, in the early eighties, had added two wings at right angles to the south front, so that the old 'circle' before the front door became a grassy court."[29] Architecture stayed with her to the end.

In May 1937, Edith, making her way to St.-Brice, stopped at Ogden Codman's Château de Grégy in Brie-Comte-Robert, for a visit and to discuss a new edition of *The Decoration of Houses*. Ogden pretentiously claimed: "It still seems to me a book that most architects and *all their clients* should buy—*To read, mark, learn, inwardly digest and profit thereby*." An inexpensive edition, he wrote, would put the book within everybody's reach.[30] Edith arrived and collapsed; the doctor diagnosed a stroke and ordered an ambulance to take her back to St.-Brice, where she died on August 11. Her burial took place at the nearby Cimetière des Gonards in Versailles. Codman true to form complained about the disruption to his planned social schedule: "it has been no joke putting up all her people . . . Everyone was on the jump all the time." He worried about having to rearrange carefully orchestrated lunches and dinners.[31] Ogden's petulance could have become an amusing incident—complete with an architectural setting—for a story.

NOTES

CHAPTER 1
Finding Her Way

1. Edith Wharton, *A Backward Glance* (New York: D. Appleton & Co., 1934), 125.
2. Quoted in Percy Lubbock, *Portrait of Edith Wharton* (London: Jonthan Cape, 1947) 129-30.
3. Lubbock, *Portrait*, 34-35.
4. Wharton, *The House of Mirth* (New York: Charles Scribner's Sons, 1905), 39.
5. Wharton, *A Backward Glance*, 28.
6. Wharton and Ogden Codman Jr., *The Decoration of Houses* (New York: Charles Scribner's Sons, 1897), 198.
7. Wharton, "The Angel at the Grave" (1900), in *Roman Fever and Other Stories* (New York: Scribner Paperback Fiction, 1997), 134, 137 and *A Backward Glance*, 125.
8. Wharton, *The Writing of Fiction* (New York: Charles Scribner's Sons, 1925), 85.
9. For background I have relied upon R. W. B. Lewis, *Edith Wharton: A Biography* (New York: Harper & Row, 1975); Eleanor Dwight, *Edith Wharton: An Extraordinary Life* (New York: Abrams, 1994); Hermione Lee, *Edith Wharton* (New York: Random House, 2007); Louis Auchincloss, *Edith Wharton: A Woman in Her Time* (New York, Viking Press, 1971); and Barbara L. Kernan, "Edith in the Art and 'Act of Making Habitation for Herself,'" PhD. diss. University of Wisconsin-Madison, 2008.
10. Vincent Scully, *The Shingle Style and The Stick Style*, rev. ed. (New Haven: Yale University Press, 1971). Pencraig was demolished in the 1910s, and its architect remains unknown, though the house bears some resemblance to the work of Richard Morris Hunt and/or John Hubbard Sturgis.
11. Wharton, "Life And I," in *Novellas and Other Writings* (New York: Library of America, 1990), 1072.
12. Wharton, *A Backward Glance,* 44, 54, 55.
13. Wharton, "A Little Girl's New York," *Harper's* 176 (March 1938), 361, 358.
14. Wharton, *A Backward Glance*, 52; Lewis, *Wharton*, 43.
15. Wharton, *A Backward Glance*, 91.
16. Wharton, "Life and I," 1087.
17. Henry James, letter to Howard Sturgis, February 22, 1912, quoted in Millicent Bell, *Edith Wharton & Henry James* (New York: Braziller, 1965), 180.
18. Wharton, *The Cruise of the Vanadis*, Claudine Lesage, ed. (New York: Rizzoli, 2003), 71.
19. Meryle Secrest, *Being Bernard Berenson: A Biography* (New York: Holt, Rinehart Winston, 1979) and *The Letters of Bernard Berenson and Isabella Stewart Gardner 1887–1924*, R. van Hadley, ed. (Boston: Northeastern University Press, 1987).
20. Vineta Colby, *Vernon Lee: A Literary Biography* (Charlottesville: University of Virginia Press, 2003).
21. Wharton, *A Backward Glance*, 149.
22. Bernard Berenson, *The Venetian Painters* (1894), reprinted in *The Italian Painters of the Renaissance* (Cleveland, 1957), iii. For background see Richard Guy Wilson, Dianne Pilgrim, and Richard Murray, *The American Renaissance 1876–1917* (New York: Brooklyn Museum of Art and Pantheon Books, 1979).
23. Charles Moore, *The Life and Times of Charles Follen McKim* (New York: Houghton Mifflin Co., 1929), 260.
24. Moore, *McKim*, 161, 168.
25. Wharton, *A Backward Glance*, 92-95, 149; Lewis, *Edith Wharton*, 56; Lee, *Wharton*, 68-71.

26. [George William Sheldon] *Artistic Houses* (New York: D. Appleton & Co., 1883-84), vol. 1, pt. 2, 135. See also Arnold Lewis, James Turner, and Steven McQuillin, *The Opulent Interiors of the Gilded Age: All 203 Photographs from "Artistic Houses" with New Text* (New York: Dover, 1987), 70-71 and Paul R. Baker, *Richard Morris Hunt* (Cambridge: MIT Press, 1980), 230.

27. Wharton, *A Backward Glance*, 92-94.

28. Wharton, *The Age of Innocence*, 309.

29. "Schoolroom Decoration," *Newport Daily News,* October 8, 1897, reprinted in *Edith Wharton, The Uncollected Critical Writings*, Frederic Wegener, ed. (Princeton: Princeton University Press, 1996), 58.

30. Wharton, *A Backward Glance*, 106.

31. Wharton, *French Ways and Their Meaning* (New York: D. Appleton & Co., 1919), 43.

32. Ogden Codman to Arthur Little, August 17, 1891, Historic New England.

33. For Codman, see Pauline Metcalf, ed., *Ogden Codman and the Decoration of Houses* (Boston: The Boston Athenaeum and David R. Godine, 1988), chapters 1, 2, 4.

34. Wharton, Letter to Ogden Codman, April 30, 1897, Historic New England. Land's End survives but it has been drastically remodeled and very little of the Codman-Wharton house remains.

35. Wharton, *A Backward Glance*, 106

36. *Decoration*, 115.

37. EW to OC, n.d. (c. 1893), Historic New England.

38. Wharton, "The Valley of Childish Things, and Other Emblems," *The Century* 52 (July 1896): 467-69.

39. Wharton, "The Fullness of Life," *Scribner's* 14 (December 1893), 700; reprinted in *The Collected Short Stories of Edith Wharton* 14. See also Susan Fraiman, "Domesticity beyond Sentiment: Edith Wharton, Decoration, and Divorce," *American Literature* 83 (September 2011), 479-507.

40. "Newport's Old Houses" *Newport Daily News,* January 8, 1896, reprinted in *Uncollected Critical Writings*, 58. McKim's observation appears in *New York Sketch Book of Architecture* 1:12 (December 1874), op pl. 45.

41. EW to OC, April 17, 1896, Historic New England.

42. EW to OC [Milan], April 23 [1895], Historic New England.

43. OC to Sarah Bradlee Codman, December 13, 1893, Historic New England.

44. Charles McKim to OC, February 19, March 31, April 9, 1897, Library of Congress. See also Katherine Boyd Menz and Donald McTernan, "Decorating for the Frederick Vanderbilts," *Nineteenth Century* 3 (Winter 1977): 44-50.

45. Wharton, *A Backward Glance*, 107.

46. Florence Codman, *The Clever Young Boston Architect* (Augusta, Maine: Privately printed, 1970), 2.

47. Wharton, *A Backward Glance*, 107-8.

48. EW to Charles McKim, Wednesday [January 1897], New York Public Library.

49. EW to OC, Saturday [February 1897], Historic New England.

50. EW to OC, February 20, 1897, Historic New England.

51. Wharton, *A Backward Glance*, 108.

52. EW to OC, May 9, 1897, Historic New England.

53. Wharton, *A Backward Glance*, 110.

54. The original fifty-six plates appeared in all the reprintings during Wharton's lifetime. Unfortunately, the W. W. Norton reprinting for Classical America substituted new photographs. The most recent reprinting by Rizzoli contains the original plates.

55. Daniel Marot, *Das Ornamentwerk de Daniel Marot* (Berlin, Ernst Wasmuth, 1892), pl. 29. Updike's participation is recorded in Lubbock, *Portrait*, 18.

56. EW to OC, n.d. [1897 is written on the letter], Historic New England.

57. EW to OC, n.d., Historic New England.

58. EW to OC, Thursday [June 1897], Historic New England.

59. EW to OC, November 9, 1897, Historic New England.

60. EW to OC, Saturday [c. February 6, 1897], Historic New England.

61. The reply by McKim is a three-page typed "memoranda" with "to Mrs. Wharton" penciled in on the first page. Bound into his letter copy book; the surrounding letters are dated February 2 and 5, 1897. Library of Congress. McKim would have sent the original to Wharton, but it has not survived.

62. Andrew Jackson Downing, *The Architecture of Country Houses* (New York: 1850); and Marianna Griswold Van Rensselaer, "Recent Architecture in the United States, VI City Dwellings II," *Century Magazine* 31 (March 1886), 685-86.

63. *Decoration,* 4, 77, 8, 49, 58, 82.

64. *Decoration*, xix.

65. *Decoration*, 198.

66. *Decoration*, 6-8, xix, pls. II and IV. See also Joan DeJean, *The Age of Comfort* (New York: Bloomsbury, 2009).

67. *Decoration*, pls. XLI and XLII.

68. *Decoration*, xx, 128, 117, 2, 9, 28. See Carroll L. V. Meeks, "Picturesque Eclecticism," *Art Bulletin* 32 (September 1950), 226-35.

69. Wharton, *A Backward Glance*, 140-41; Wharton, "A Tuscan Shrine," *Scribner's* 17 (January 1895), 22-32, reprinted in Wharton, *Italian Backgrounds* (New York: Charles Scribner's Sons, 1905), 83-104.

70. *Decoration*, 34, 31.

71. *Decoration*, 196, 198, 175.

72. I owe this observation to Scott Marshall.

73. *The Nation* 65 (December 16, 1897), 485.

74. *Advertiser* (Boston), December 21, 1897, clipping in Codman files, Historic New England.

75. E. B. B., "A new Book on Interior Decoration," *Architectural Review* [Boston] 5 (March 10, 1989), 20; "Literature: Hints for Home Decoration," *The Critic*, April 1898, 161; and *Book Buyer* 16 (March 1898), 129.

76. "Have Art with Comfort at Home," *New York Herald,* January 23, 1898.

77. Walter Berry, "The Decoration of Houses," *The Bookman* 7 (April 1898), 161-63.

78. "Books and Papers," *American Architect* 59 (January 22, 1899): 28.

79. The book was reprinted in London by B. T. Batsford in 1898 and in New York by Scribner's in 1902 and 1919.

80. W. J. Loftie to EW, January 3, 1898; and Reginald Blomfield to EW, January 20, 1898, Historic New England.

81. Wharton, *A Backward Glance,* 125; and EW to OC, May 2, 1897, Historic New England.

82. EW to OC, August 1, 1900, Historic New England.

CHAPTER 2
Designing and Building The Mount

1. Wharton, *A Backward Glance*, 124-25.

2. Lewis, *Wharton*, 93, 100, 110; Lee, *Wharton*, 136-38; Scott Marshall, *The Mount: Home of Edith Wharton* (Lenox: Edith Wharton Restoration, Inc., 1997), chapter 4.

3. *Lenox Life*, May 25, 1901, 3.

4. *Lenox Life*, August 17, 1901, 3.

5. Marshall, *Mount*, 51.

6. EW to OC, July 11, 1899; July 1900; September 9, 1901; Historic New England.

7. *Decoration*, 4.

8. Clive Aslet, *The American Country House* (New Haven: Yale University Press, 1990); Mark Alan Hewitt, *The Architect & the American Country House* (New Haven: Yale University Press, 1990); Roger W. Moss, *The American Country House* (New York: Holt, 1990); Richard Guy Wilson and Steven Bedford, *The Long Island Country House* exh. cat. (Southampton: Parrish Art Museum, 1988); Robert B. MacKay, Anthony Baker, and Carol A. Traynor, eds., *Long Island Country Houses and Their Architects, 1860-1940* (New York: W. W. Norton, 1997).

9. OC to Sarah Fletcher Bradlee Codman, February 25, 1901, Historic New England.

10. OC to Sarah Fletcher Bradlee Codman, March 9, 1901, Historic New England.

11. OC to Sarah Fletcher Bradlee Codman, February 25 and March 19, 1901, Historic New England.

12. EW to OC, March 25, 1901, Historic New England.

13. OC to Sarah Fletcher Bradlee Codman, March 25 and July 1, 1901, Historic New England.

14. EW to OC, June 30, 1897, Historic New England.

15. Richard Guy Wilson, *Harbor Hill: Portrait of a House* (New York: W. W. Norton, 2008).

16. Francis L. V. Hoppin, "An Architectural Knockabout," *American Architect and Building News* 26 (July 6, July 13, August 3, August 10, August 17, August 24, August 31, 1889), 3-5, 15-16, 48-50, 61, 74-75, 89-91, 96-97. For information on Hoppin I am indebted to Stuart Siegel, "The Architecture of Hoppin & Koen," draft graduate

thesis, University of Virginia.

17. OC to Sarah Fletcher Bradlee Codman, July 1, 1900, Historic New England.

18. "'The Mount,' In Lenox," *Berkshire Resort Topics* II, no. 10 (Sept 1904), 1.

19. "Three Houses at Aiken, F. C. Hoppin & Koen, Architect," *Architectural Review* [Boston] 9 (September 1902), 114.

20. [H. Avary Tipping] "Belton House, Grantham," *Country Life* 4 (September 24 and October 1, 1898, 368-72, 400-3; reprinted in [H. Avary Tipping] *English Homes* (London: Country Life, 1904), vol. 1, 1-9. Tipping claims Wren as the architect. Colin Campbell, *Vitruvius Britannicus, or the British Architect* (London, 1715), vol. 2, pl.37, 38. John Cornforth, "Belton House, Lincolnshire," *Country Life* 136 (September 3, 10, 17, 1964), 562-65, 620-24, 700-3, identifies William Winde as the architect and William Stanton as the builder.

21. Henry James, *The American Scene* (New York: Harper & Bros., 1907), 38-39.

22. Drawings for The Mount are in the Avery Architectural and Fine Arts Library, Columbia University, and also at The Mount.

23. OC to Sarah Fletcher Bradlee Codman, January 1, 1902, Historic New England.

24. OC to Sarah Fletcher Bradlee Codman, October 27, 1901, Historic New England.

25. OC to Sarah Fletcher Bradlee Codman, March 24 and March 14, 1902, Historic New England.

26. EW to OC, December 31, 1901, Historic New England. Amelia Alexandra Peck, "Restoration Plan for the Interior of the Mount, Lenox, Massachusetts," MA Thesis Columbia University, 1984, provides valuable information on the interior.

27. Wharton, *A Backward Glance*, 110.

28. *Decoration*, 17.

29. *Decoration*, 138, 117.

30. "'The Mount,' In Lenox" *Berkshire Resort Topics* II, no. 10 (September 1904), 1, provides a description of the furnishings.

31. *Decoration*, 38.

32. *Decoration,* 38 and 123-26.

33. Henry James to Jessie Allen, October 22, 1904, in *Henry James–Letters* (Cambridge: Belknap Press of Harvard University Press, 1984) IV, 329.

34. *Decoration*, 151-152, 153.

35. Marshall, *Mount,* 79.

36. "'The Mount,' In Lenox," *Berkshire Resort Topics.*

37. EW to OC, c. 1901, Historic New England.

38. *Decoration*, 150

39. *Decoration*, 159

40. *Decoration*, 171.

41. Mrs. Gordon Bell, quoted in Lubbock, *Portrait*, 35.

42. *Decoration*, 130, 131.

43. On conditions, see John G. Waite Associates, "Part Two, Existing Conditions…" in Marshall, *Mount.*

44. OC to Sarah Fletcher Bradlee Codman, October 8, 1902, Historic New England.

45. *Berkshire Resort Topics* II, no. 10 (September 10, 1904), 1.

46. Matilda Gay, quoted in Historic Structure Report for the Stable, Claude Emmanuel Menders Architects, Inc., 2001, 14.

47. David H. Bennett, "Sensations of the Unexpected" in *Edith Wharton and the American Garden* (Lenox: Mount Press, 2009), 43.

48. Information from Scott Marshall, June 1987.

49. "Garden Books in Edith Wharton's Library" a list compiled by Betsy Anderson, The Mount archives.

50. EW to George B. Dorr, September 3, 1904, Beinecke Library, Yale University.

51. EW to OC, August 1, 1900, Historic New England.

52. Wharton, "The Duchess at Prayer," *Scribner's* 28 (August 1900), 155.

53. Wharton, *Italian Villas and Their Gardens*, New York: The Century Co., 1904), v.

54. Wharton, *Italian Villas*, 5, 56

55. Charles Adams Platt, "Italian Gardens," *Harper's New Monthly Magazine,* 87 (July, August, 1893), 165-180, 393-406; Platt, *Italian Gardens* (New York: Harper, 1894). See also Keith Morgan, *Charles Adams Platt* (Cambridge: MIT Press, 1985)

56. Wharton, *Italian Villas*, 46.

57. EW Diary, Beinecke Library, Yale University.

58. Hildegarde Hawthorne, *The Lure of the Garden* (New York: The Century Co., 1911), 135.

CHAPTER 3
Life at The Mount

1. Quoted in Lewis, *Wharton*, 111.
2. Lee, *Wharton*, 140.
3. Wharton, *A Backward Glance*, 143, 124, 106; Wharton, "The Line of Least Resistance," *Lippincott's Magazine* 66 (October 1900), 559-70; and "The Twilight of the Gods," in Wharton, *The Greater Inclination* (New York: Scribner's, 1899).
4. Wharton, *A Backward Glance,* 293-94.
5. Richard Guy Wilson, *The Colonial Revival House* (New York: Abrams, 2004), 16.
6. Raymond DeWitt Mallary, *Lenox and the Berkshire Highlands* (New York: Putnam, 1902), 83.
7. Mallary, 83.
8. On the Berkshires as a summer resort see: Richard S. Jackson Jr. and Cornelia Brooke Gilder, *Houses of the Berkshires: 1870-1930* (New York: Acanthus Press, 2006); Cleveland Amory, *The Last Resorts* (New York: Grosset & Dunlap, 1952); Donald T. Oaks, ed., *A Pride of Palaces: Lenox Summer Cottages, 1883-1933* (Lenox: Lenox Library Association, 1981); *Picturesque Berkshire* (Northampton, Mass. Picturesque Perkshire Pub. Co., 1893); *The Berkshire Hills: A WPA Guide* (Boston: Northeastern University Press, 1939, 1987); Carole Owens, *The Berkshire Cottages* (Lenox: Cottage Press, 1984).
9. "Correspondence," *American Architect and Building News* 2, no. 102 (December 9, 1877), 394.
10. Henry James, *The American Scene*, 40, 48.
11. Honey Sharp, "Edith Wharton: An Encounter with the Berkshires," in *Edith Wharton and the American Garden*, 35.
12. *Decoration*, 126.
13. Owens, *Berkshire Cottages,* 88.
14. *Lenox Life,* July 6, 1901, 4.
15. *Lenox Life,* June 2, 1900, 1.
16. Updike quoted in Lubbock, *Portrait*, 29.
17. Lee, *Wharton*, 72.
18. Gaillard Lapsley, "E. W." (ms) 26-27 in Yale Collection of American Literature, Beinecke Rare Book and Manuscript Library, Yale University. See also, Lee, *Wharton*, 81.
19. Marshall, *The Mount*, 149; and EW to Morton Fullerton, June 8-11, 1908, in Lewis, *Letters*, 152
20. Lee, *Wharton*, 527.

21. EW to Morton Fullerton, July 3, 1911, in Lewis, *Letters*, 242.
22. Lee, *Wharton*, 38, 148, 182, 422, 480; Lewis, *Wharton*, 150; Wharton "Life and I," 1081.
23. Wharton, *A Backward Glance*, 124.
24. Henry James to Howard Sturgis, October 17, 1904, in *Henry James Letters*, L. Edel, ed., (Cambridge: Harvard University Press, 1984), vol. 1, 325.
25. Lubbock, *Portrait*, 82.
26. Wendy Baker, David Bennett, and Diane Derkes, A Landscape Architecture Analysis and Master Plan for The Mount. Prepared for the Massachusetts Council on the Arts and Humanities, Edith Wharton Restoration, Inc., and Shakespeare & Company, Harvard Graduate School of Design, 1982.
27. "The Lenox Cottagers," *Berkshire Resort Topics*, August 6, 1904, 6; Lewis, *Wharton*, 147; *Lenox Life*, August 6, 1904, 6.
28. Helen and Mary MacDonald, *A History of the Lenox Library* (Lenox: Lenox Library, 1956).
29. Edith Wharton, *Summer*; a novel (New York, D. Appleton and Company, 1917), 13, 18.
30. EW to Sara Norton, July 18, 1904, Beinecke Library, Yale University.
31. Marshall, *Mount*, 58.
32. EW to Helen Brice, August 13, 1903, The Mount archives.
33. Obituary of Richard T. Auchmuty, *New York Times*, July 19, 1893.
34. Wharton, *A Backward Glance*, 294.
35. Lapsley, "E.W.," 17.
36. Marshall, *Mount,* 148.
37. *Lenox Life*, October 5, 1901, 4; and September 20, 1902, np; and Marshall, *Mount*, 58.
38. *Lenox Life*, May 26, 1900, 1.
39. Wharton, *A Backward Glance*, 153.
40. Wharton, *A Backward Glance*, 296.
41. James to William James, July 2, 1905, in Percy Lubbock, *Letters of Henry James,* (Macmillan & Scribners, 1920), vol. II, 36.
42. Wharton, *A Backward Glance,* 153.
43. Wesley S. Griswold, "Mrs. Wharton's 'Cook,'" *Hartford Courant*, September 19, 1937, D4.
44. *Lenox Life*, August 17, 1901, 4.
45. *Lenox Life*, July 6, 1901, 4.
46. Lapsley, "E.W." 17.
47. Lee, *Wharton*, 153-155; Lewis, *Wharton*, 147-149; Marshall, *Mount*, 171, n77 lists names from local newspapers and other sources of who stayed at the Mount.

48. Wharton, *A Backward Glance*, 185.

49. Lubbock, *Portrait*, 77.

50. Lee, *Wharton*, 153.

51. Quoted in Lee, *Wharton*, 153.

52. Mrs. Daniel Chester French, *Memories of a Sculptor's Wife* (Boston: Houghton Mifflin, 1928), 206.

53. D. C. French to EW, November 12, 1906, copy in The Mount archives.

CHAPTER 4
Afterward

1. Wharton, *A Backward Glance,* 125.

2. OC to Sarah Codman, December 19, 1902, Historic New England.

3. Lewis, *Wharton*, 192; Lee, *Edith Wharton*, 312, 338, 364-370.

4. Quoted in Lewis, *Wharton*, 183.

5. James to William James, July 2, 1905, in Percy Lubbock, *Letters of Henry James*, (New York: MacMillan & Scribner's, 1920), vol. II, 36.

6. Lewis, *Wharton,* 191.

7. *Town Topics*, August 10, 1911.

8. EW to Bernard Berenson, August 6, 1911, Beinecke Library, Yale Univeristy.

9. Henry James to EW, July 19, 1911, quoted in Lyall H. Powers, ed., *Henry James and Edith Wharton Letters: 1900–1915* (New York: Scribner's, 1990), 182.

10. Marshall, *Mount*, 124-25.

11. "Shattuck Buys the Wharton Property," *The Berkshire Evening Eagle,* September 11, 1911, 6.

12. EW to Morton Fullerton, September 22, 1911, in Lewis ed., *Letters*, 255-56.

13. Lee, *Wharton*, 400-401

14. EW to Gaillard Lapsley, August 19, 1912, in Lewis, ed., *Letters*, 277.

15. "Albert Shattuck Dies at his Villa in Lenox," *Berkshire Evening Eagle*, November 5, 1925, 15. Except where noted, most of the information on the subsequent ownership of the Mount after the Whartons' occupancy comes from Marshall, *Mount*, chapter 8, and information in The Mount archives.

16. "Sale of Jewels, Furniture and Objets d'Art of the Late Mrs. Shattuck . . ." *Berkshire Evening Eagle*, October 22, 1935, quoted in Marshall, *Mount*, 128

17. "Foxhollow School Buys the Mount, Lenox," *Springfield Daily Republican*, August 18, 1942, copy in The Mount archives.

18. Wharton, *A Backward Glance*, 28.

19. Wharton, "A Little Girl's New York," *Harper's* 176 (March 1938), 357.

20. Wharton, *Italian Backgrounds*, 177.

21. EW to Sara Norton quoted in Lewis, *Wharton*, 143.

22. Wharton, *French Ways*, 38-40.

23. Wharton, *The Age of Innocence* (New York: D. Appleton, 1920), 349, 347.

24. Wharton, "New Year's Day," in *Old New York* (New York: Scribner's, 1920), 296.

25. Wharton, *The Age of Innocence*, 71-72.

26. EW to Gaillard Lapsley, February 11, 1928, Beinecke Library, Yale University.

27. EW to Robert Grant, February 10, 1928, Beinecke Library, Yale University.

28. Wharton, *A Backward Glance,* 125.

29. Edith Wharton, "All Souls" (1937), in *The Selected Short Stories of Edith Wharton*, R. W. B. Lewis, ed., (New York: Scribner's, 1991), 367-68.

30. OC to EW, April 18, 1937, Historic New England.

31. OC to Thomas Newbold Codman, June 5, 1937; and OC to Julian Sampson, June 4, 1937, Boston Athenaeum.

INDEX
Numbers in *italic* refer to illustrations

CREDITS

Photographs by John Arthur except as noted below:

Avery Architectural and Fine Arts Library, Columbia University: 49, 56, 57

David Dashiell: 10-11, 40, 41, 67, 75, 80, 86, 94, 96-97, 99

Dumbarton Oaks, Research Library and Collections, Washington, D. C.,
gift of Louisa Farrand Wood: 27

Edith Wharton Restoration Archives: 51, 54, 64, 65, 136

Environmental Design Archives, Beatrix Farrand Collection (1955-2), University
of California, Berkeley: 98

Great Houses of the Berkshires: 131, 133, 140 top

Historic New England: 25, 28, 29, 30

Knickerbocker Club, New York: 22

Lenox Library Association, Lenox, Massachusetts: 9, 37, 126, 141 top, 143

Library of Congress: 36, 153 right

Lilly Library, Indiana University, Bloomington, Indiana: 146

National Portrait Gallery, Smithsonian Institution, Washington, D. C.: 14

Private Collection: 23

Yale Collection of American Literature, Beinecke Rare Book and Manuscript Library: 1, 7,
13, 15, 16, 17, 18, 19, 20, 21, 26, 32, 33, 45, 46-47, 68, 72, 78, 82, 84, 100, 110, 115, 116, 129,
135, 141 bottom, 144, 145, 147, 148, 149, 152, 153 left, 155, 159, 161, 162, 163

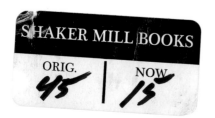